FAITH, HOPE AND LOVE

THE PILLARS OF
PROGRESSIVE CHRISTIANITY

*"Progressive Christianity is neither new or old
but rather a Faith built on sound
and solid principles for the ages."*

FRED C. PLUMER, PRESIDENT
THE CENTER FOR PROGRESSIVE CHRISTIANITY

To Bev, Sean, Joanie, Isabella and Cameron...
With Lots of Faith for the Family of Man.

FAITH, HOPE AND LOVE

THE PILLARS OF PROGRESSIVE CHRISTIANITY

GARY ALAN WILBURN

with

GAIL WHITCOME LINSTROM

PROGRESSIVEPUB

Stamford, CT

ISBN: 978-0-9701374-4-9

ProgressivePub
Stamford, CT
For information, email contactus@ProgressivePub.com

Cover art by Sean Wilburn and Kent La Gree
Sean@ProgressivePub.com and kent@lagreephotography.com

Back cover photo of Gary A. Wilburn by Peter Hanson

Book design by Cheryl Mirkin,
CMF Graphic Design

Printed in the United States of America

CONTENTS

ACKNOWLEDGEMENTS

I wish to thank my publisher and friend Meyrick Payne of ProgressivePub, without whose encouragement there would have been no books, my editor Gail Linstrom who became my co-author and hands in compiling this book, my graphic designer Cheryl Mirkin of CMF Graphic Design who as always has turned a rough manuscript into a professional publication, my son, Sean Wilburn of Wilburn Consulting for his cover design, and my wife, Bev, who has been my partner in ministry and life and has become my voice. I owe a special debt of gratitude to my long-time friend Ken Watts whose excitement over my pamphlet explaining Progressive Christianity inspired the vision for this book.

*A plaque which hangs in Gary and Bev's Baja home
that was a 2009 Christmas gift from the La Mision Community
to their friend and "pastor in residence."*

PREFACE

It was a weekend in mid-June, 2010. Gary Wilburn knew that his earthly battle with ALS was near its end. The house in Playa La Mision, Baja California, was full of family and close friends that had come to say good-bye. There were tears, but there was the laughter and fullness of life that so characterized the man that we had come to know and love so dearly. He was spending his last days just as he had lived his life, savoring each moment, living each day with love and hope, rather than fear and anxiety. It turned out this would be just two weeks before Gary would slip into the arms of the God he loved on June 28.

It was in this time that Gary unselfishly embarked on assembling this last book for those seekers of the twenty-first century who are struggling "to open [themselves] up to an emerging faith which finds more grace in the search for meaning than in absolute certainty, and more life in the questions than in the answers." Ministers are generally known for either having a gift for administration, teaching, preaching, or pastoring. Those of us who were fortunate to be congregants of Gary were blessed with a leader who served his churches well in each of these areas. But most of all, Gary was a rare breed that was equally strong as a teacher and a pastor to congregants and friends alike. He suddenly realized that his trilogy on Faith, Hope, and Love—*The God I Don't Believe In: Charting a New Course for Christianity, Lots of Hope,* and *Lots of Love*—pastored us in our search because he was here to walk beside us. He knew that we would need some solid teaching to guide us in our journey.

As Tina McMurry, a very long-time friend, wrote on CaringBridge.com, "My steps forward have been because Gary put a pebble for me to follow. One pebble . . . See here, where this leads. Another pebble . . . Now you are ready to see where this leads. Still another . . . This is a hard path, but it opens to a beautiful meadow. None of this was purposed by you; it was rather just you being you. A natural travel through city, jungle, desert. As you went through your path to great change and understanding of faith, many of us, not just me, found our path well lit and clearer to follow." But Gary knew that he would no longer be here to put out the pebbles for us. We would need something tangible to guide us on our way.

Gary chose the eight points developed by the Center for Progressive Christianity to build his book around and to illuminate that road. He firmly believed in each of these precepts and has used them to show us how we can be inclusive of all humanity. He offers us practical yet inspirational ways to translate our personal faith in Jesus into a journey of Love that empowers us to serve the whole of humanity. Gary constantly reminded us that Jesus's two great commandments were to "Love the Lord your God with all of your HEART and all of your SOUL and all of your MIND" and "Love your neighbor as yourselves." For Gary, there were no ifs, ands, or buts about it, and he did not hesitate to tell us so.

Here I offer you Gary's last book so that you can be part of the journey, putting feet to your faith as you live passionately. As his wife Bev observed, Gary approached each day as a new adventure. I thank Gary for his confidence in me and for this last gift that inspires us to open our minds and hearts to live reflecting the love of Jesus and challenges us to tear down monuments to indifference, greed, or inhumanity in our own hearts and in society.

Humbly with passion for the journey,
Gail W. Linstrom
Editor, Former Congregant, and Friend
Gail@ProgressivePub.com

FORWARD

"Faith is the assurance of things hoped for,
the conviction of things not seen."
—HEBREWS 1:11

This book is my fourth intended to complement the Trilogy on Faith, Hope, and Love. My first book, *The God I Don't Believe In: Charting a New Course for Christianity*, focused on my profound belief that we need to take a new look at Christianity and our faith. *Lots of Hope* was intended to give courage to those who dedicate their lives and live in ways which reflect how the world should be according to the precepts of our faith, and not how it is. In *Lots of Love* I wanted to lend strength to those who desire to extricate themselves from the fear that overrules their faith and to assure them that "the greatest of these is Love." Now I want to give you a roadmap for your journey and inspire you as you live out your faith putting into practice the concepts introduced in the trilogy and the precepts of Progressive Christianity.

There are eight points that have been researched, refined, and articulated by the Center for Progressive Christianity as guidelines for those Christians and churches who want to expand their view of the world and of their faith following a path of inclusiveness rather than exclusivity. By calling ourselves progressive, we mean that we are Christians who: (1) Have found an approach to God through the life and teachings of Jesus. (2) Recognize the faithfulness of other people who have other names for the way to God's realm, and acknowledge that their ways are true for them, as our ways are true for us. (3) Understand the sharing of bread and wine in Jesus's name to be a representation of an ancient vision of God's people for all peoples. (4) Invite all people to participate in our community and worship life without insisting that they become like us in order to be acceptable (including . . . but not limited to): believers and agnostics, conventional Christians and questioning skeptics, women and men, those of all sexual orientations and gender identities, those of all races and cultures, those of all classes and abilities, those who hope for a better world and those who have lost hope. (5) Know that the way we act toward one another and toward other people is the fullest expression of what we believe. (6) Find more grace in the search for understanding than we do in dogmatic certainty—more value in questioning than in absolutes. (7) Form ourselves into communities dedicated to equipping one another for the work we feel called to do: striving for peace and justice among all people, protecting and restoring the integrity of all God's creation, and bringing hope to those Jesus called the least of his brothers and sisters. (8) Recognize that being followers of Jesus is costly, and entails selfless love, conscientious resistance to evil, and renunciation of privilege.[1]

This will be my last book. In 2007 I was diagnosed most unexpectedly as having Amyotrophic Lateral Sclerosis (ALS), or Lou Gehrig's disease. ALS is a progressive disease that attacks the body's motor neurons, leading to loss of muscle control, paralysis, and untimely death. Typically, ALS patients live two to five years after diagnosis. At present, there is still no known cause nor cure for this disease. Since that time I have lived each day as an adventure, filled with hope and love and laughter as well as shedding a few tears. Although I recognize that I am nearing the end of my earthly life, I still have that faith and hope and love. But this is not the end of the story . . . this is the beginning of the cure. I have Faith that cures will be ultimately developed, not in time for me, but for others who contract this horrible disease, and others like it, after me.

Have ... LOTS OF FAITH ... HOPE ... and LOVE,
Gary

INTRODUCTION

AN APPROACH TO GOD THROUGH JESUS

"They were astounded at [Jesus's] teaching, for
he taught them as one having authority."
—MARK 1:22

If ever there was a time when children, young people, moms and dads, single and partnered people need to experience a new vitality in their religion, it is now. People are yearning to define their values and their identity in a society where many of the key institutions that used to provide them—family, churches, and political leaders—seem to be in flux or under siege. Change bombards us, and in the race to keep up with that change many people feel they are losing a sense of who they are. I believe that the tenets of Progressive Christianity provide the pathway to discovering the answers to those questions and embracing life-giving faith today.

The world is experiencing turmoil akin to that of the first century. We as Christians are thrust into the struggle to interpret our faith against strong political, social, and moral forces all competing for our loyalty. We thought our religion provided a framework from which to evaluate our decisions. Now it sometimes seems irrelevant. Things are changing so quickly, not just in our country but worldwide, as questions about lifestyle, values, social issues, and justice assault us. How do we reconcile the world and facts we thought we knew within the context of the new world that is emerging?

Life for us today is much as it was for Jesus's followers in the days immediately following Jesus's death and resurrection. Theirs was a new reality against which they had to adapt their old life and assumptions. It was then that the early Christians banded together in spontaneous, non-institutional communities to share and interpret their new-found faith. Luke reports that they worshipped in their Jewish temples and synagogues every morning (since most of them were Jewish), and in their Christian homes every evening—young and old alike—grandparents, parents, and children around the family table.

Their common life was shaped by testimonials and teaching, by fellowship, worship, sharing, and caring. They did not "join a church," as we know it. The experience of having their lives changed in lasting and decisive ways by the love of God drew them to one another, and to those outside the community, with a desire to share with others the overwhelming, overflowing love of God.

So today how do we take seriously the experience of our faith and share our newly-awakened lives with others? For some Christians, the only choice has been between fundamentalism and secularism. I believe that choice is a false and negative one. As the members of my New Canaan church—where I last served as an active pastor—found and practice, there is more grace in the search for meaning than in absolute certainty, in the questions than in the answers. As a church, this specific congregation has become a "spiritual home" for a number of folks of other faiths (and none).

The Mission Statement of the First Presbyterian Church in New Canaan, Connecticut, is "To Live Spiritually, To Love Inclusively, To Learn Continuously, and To Leave a Legacy." That statement of core values embraces the principles of Progressive Christianity. It has helped its members over the years to "flesh out," as it were, their faith and their responsibilities as a church. For individuals the question is, "What do we mean when we say we are Progressive Christians and how do we live our lives to reflect our beliefs?"

Progressive Christians take part in a Christ-centered faith. Like those early Christians, they gather together to try to make some sense of their experience of resurrection. Like many, they have some religious yearning that cannot be adequately expressed in an ancient creed or confession, or in a Bible verse. They believe in thinking and want to think in believing. So, while they proclaim Jesus Christ as the Gate to the realm of God, they also recognize the faithfulness of other people who have other names for the gateway to God's realm.[2] We are constantly looking for ways to approach truth which are open, exciting, and fluid, and yet faithful to the basic tenets of the Christian gospel.

As Christians, we find the revelation of God primarily in a person, an affirmation unique among the major religions of the world. This does not make Christianity superior, but does make it different. We believe that in Jesus, "the word became flesh and lived among us," as the Bible puts it.[3] This is the central meaning of incarnation: Jesus is the "Face of God" for Christians. Jesus is what can be seen of God embodied in a human life. Jesus shows us what God is like and what God is most passionate about.

As Mark, the Gospel writer closest to the memories of the life of Jesus, wrote, "They were astounded at [Jesus's] teaching, for he taught them as one having authority." As Marcus Borg puts it: "Jesus shows us the heart of God . . . Jesus trumps the Bible; when they disagree, Jesus wins."[4]

The key truth here is that "For us, God is defined by Jesus, but not confined to Jesus." (Bill Coffin) And as Episcopalian Bishop Krister Stendahl says, "We as Christians can sing our love songs to Jesus with wild abandon without needing to demean other religions."

This requires discovering an ever-new venture of faith. Ours is an expansive, not a restrictive, view of the world and of faith. We believe that a progressive faith is essential to keep us constantly moving forward, testing new thinking, and living out Christianity in new ways. Part of this journey is about celebrating the faithfulness and camaraderie of those who have other names for their ways into God's realm. As Progressive Christians, we believe that God speaks to us not only through the Biblical stories and creeds, but through all of life, especially through one another. We believe that sincere differences beautify the pattern, and that the whole human sound goes up to God in praise only from the full orchestra of humanity.

Another key point of our understanding of Christianity is this: "By calling ourselves progressive, we mean that we are Christians who understand the sharing of bread and wine in Jesus's name to be a representation of an ancient vision of God's feast for all peoples." In the Jewish Prophet Isaiah's vision of God's coming banquet, all the nations, tribes, and clans of the earth are God's guests. No one is to be excluded. Jesus acted this out in the story of his feeding the multitudes, where he laid down no conditions for participation and established no barriers to the meal. Following the example of Jesus, Progressive Christians feel that all people present should be offered bread and wine whenever the church celebrates the Lord's Supper. As we share the sacred meal together as one people, we participate in the vision of a just world where all people live at peace, where what belongs to one is shared with one's neighbor, and where no one goes hungry.

Krister Stendahl told a wonderful story about giving Holy Communion to a turbaned East Indian gentleman and afterwards asking him why one who was not a Christian had come to the table on several occasions. The man's answer was that he felt closer to God then than at any other time in his life. Who, I ask you, would refuse that man Holy Communion? This is the same story I have heard time and again of visitors' experiences in worship services with an open Communion table.

As Dietrich Bonhoeffer, whose 100th Anniversary was celebrated in 2006, put it in his poem, "Christians and Pagans":

"God goes to every man when sore distressed,
Feeds body and spirit with his bread;
For Christians, pagans alike he hangs dead,
And both alike forgiving."

How in the world of so many and varied religions can there be just one which is true? After all, "religion" (from the Latin *riligare*) means "to reconnect." In our worship we want to express the interconnectedness of all things with God as we celebrate the unity of prayer and work, healing and helping, science and faith, art and music, dance and drama, literature and liturgy, business and government, ecology and compassion, personal peace and universal wholeness. We proclaim what is true for us, while at the same time, acknowledging that other religious paths are equally true for others. By encouraging life-long learning, we ask questions. All of life's big questions are religious questions, but most of them do not have easy answers. In seeking some of these answers, we have discovered that the real key is learning how to ask the right questions.

We are called by Christ to help people look beyond private interests, nation, and race to the common good and the future of humanity and the earth. We are called to witness to divine goodness, mercy, compassion, respect for all, to name a few. Thus Progressive Christians do not seek to establish a church that is a religious club for those escaping from the world to be exclusively with their own kind. It is a place of interconnectedness, sometimes with those unlike ourselves, with whom we can "agree to disagree" and still experience a sacred "unity in diversity." As the visible Body of Christ, we have no alternative than to be fully welcoming and inclusive of all persons in the life and work of the church. In a culture which values outward appearance and success, we need to accept one another for who and what we are. We need to exhibit the kind of openness and authentic humanness that Jesus modeled and which broke down barriers of fear and built bridges of trust.

I invite you to join in the excitement and discover new possibilities for faith and life. In the following chapters it is my hope that you will meet Jesus in a fresh new way that inspires you, find new meaning in diversity, and be led to build community as way of life and an expression of your personal faith. As those early followers of Jesus said, "Come and see!" The adventure of a journey of new life awaits you.

JESUS
FOR THE
PROGRESSIVE
CHRISTIAN

CHAPTER 1

JESUS AS
THE MESSIAH

As they approached Jerusalem and came to Bethrage on the Mount of Olives, Jesus sent two disciples, saying to them, "Go to the village ahead of you, and at once you will find a donkey tied there, with her colt by her. Untie them and bring them to me. If anyone says anything to you, tell him that the Lord needs them, and he will send them right away.

This took place to fulfill what was spoken through the prophet [Zechariah]: "Say to the Daughter of Zion, 'See your king comes to you, gentle and riding on a donkey, on a colt, the foal of a donkey.'"

The disciples went and did as Jesus had instructed them. They brought the donkey and the colt, placed their cloaks on them, and Jesus sat on them. A very large crowd spread their cloaks on the road, while others cut branches from the trees and spread them on the road. The crowds that went ahead of him and those that followed shouted,

> *"Hosanna to the Son of David!"*
> *"Blessed is he who comes in the name of the Lord!"*
> *"Hosanna in the highest!"*

*When Jesus entered Jerusalem, the whole city was stirred and asked,
"Who is this?" The crowds answered, "This is Jesus, the prophet from
Nazareth in Galilee." —*MATTHEW 21:1-11

Not a few zealous Jews were prepared for a violent revolution
against Rome. When Jesus, their leader, arrived at the city gates
riding not on a grand stallion, but on a humble donkey, "the
whole city was in turmoil," asking, "Who is this?"

That question echoes down the corridors of human history.
Today, we stand at the brink of a new millennium, watching
another parade of cruise missiles, stealth aircraft, and thousand-
pound bombs pass by as thousands of crying children and fleeing
refugees are pushed along the road by tanks, in numerous countries each touched by war whether from outside forces or from
within. We do well to ask that same question today, "Who is this
on the donkey?"

The sixteenth century artist, Albrecht Durer was the first known
painter to make himself the subject of his own work. In one
famous portrait, he painted himself as Jesus, in rich robes. Was it
Jesus, or was it Durer?

Jesus Scholar, Marcus Borg, asks a similar question of Jesus.
"Could Jesus be the Messiah if he didn't think he was?" Did he
merely paint himself into the Messiah picture, as it were? Or did
he truly believe himself to be what he portrayed? Borg offers four
options:

1. Jesus thought he was the Messiah, and he was right.
2. Jesus thought he was the Messiah, and he was wrong.
3. Jesus didn't think he was the Messiah, and therefore he
   wasn't the Messiah.
4. Whether or not Jesus thought he was the Messiah, he is
   the Messiah.[5]

Many Christians choose the *first*, that Jesus believed himself to
be the Messiah of Israel, and he was right. Other Christians choose
the *fourth*, that Jesus can be the Messiah "for us," without having

believed himself to be the Messiah of God. Both of these groups believe that Jesus is the Christian Messiah. Both agree that Jesus wanted people to follow him and to take seriously what he took seriously. The key question is, "Was Jesus part of his own message? Did Jesus want people to believe *in him* (or in God alone)?"

I see it as Albert Schweitzer saw it a century ago. The best way to understand Jesus in his first century context is that he seemed to have believed that the redemption of the nation of Israel would occur, uniquely and decisively, in and through his own suffering and death. He would go through the darkest night and lead the way into the dawn of the new day. It was by taking upon himself the sins of Israel's rebellion through his death on the cross that God would bring about Israel's promised redemption.

Knowing full well what he was doing, Jesus rode into Jerusalem ahead of the nation, to fight the battle on their behalf, and to take upon himself the judgment of which he had warned, the wrath of Rome against its rebel subjects.

The final victory of God has already been won on the cross. "If the Messiah has broken through the barrier of sin that has kept Israel in exile, there is no need for anyone to remain bound any longer within the old agendas" . . . of violence, fear, and hate. Our sins, with Israel's, have been forgiven and we are set free.[6]

Dare we believe today that Jesus really did take hold of the small rudder by which the mighty ship of world history can be turned, and manage to swing it in the right direction, even though it cost him his life?

"We do not need to figure out this Jesus, let alone defend him. We need to discover afresh how to be for our world what he was for his—God's loving and subversive presence at the very heart of his bruised and bleeding world."[7]

The palms that Christians wave the world over each Palm Sunday morning are in commemoration of the day Jesus rode into Jerusalem on that donkey. The palm branch is the symbol of God's victory of humble love over the world's most violent evil. It has changed the course of nations . . . and it can save us as well.

CHAPTER 2

JESUS AS THE LORD OF LIFE

What a beautiful day Easter is in the United States! Here the warm spring sun is usually shining, the lilies are in bloom, the birds are singing, and sanctuaries are alive with the sound of music. And believers and non-believers awaken this day that is celebrated both religiously and secularly consciously aware of the love of family and friends.

It is hard to believe that tens of thousands of other families awaken in other parts of the world on such a meaningful morning without the music of Easter, dispossessed of their homes and possessions, fearful of what tragedies this same day might hold for them and their loved ones. All because of wars for which they never asked, and in which they have played no part.

Yet, there is another war that goes on, even as people worship in their churches. It is not an international conflict, but a cosmic conflict. It is a war of faith and fears. They are calling it the "Jesus Wars." At the heart of the war are symbols faithful Christians have come to love and reverence: an empty tomb and a supposed "bodily resurrection."

The first is a war for national freedom with boundaries. The second is a war for spiritual freedom without boundaries. The first war is for land and human lives. The second war is for love and human hearts. Already there have been great losses in each of the wars: losses of life and losses of faith. It is not far from the mark to speculate that if we do not win the second war, the first war will set our agenda for the millennium to come: a world without Easter.

Not one to hedge his bets, the apostle Paul, or St. Paul as he later became known, put all his Christian eggs into one Easter basket. "For if Christ has not been raised," he writes to the Corinthians, "Your faith is futile and you are still in your sins." I like the refreshing way St. Paul lays it on the line. No political double-speak, no slippery-tongued nuances, no spin-doctoring. Straight out. "Tell it like it is."

For St. Paul the light of Easter is no mere lantern swinging over a narrow, empty grave, but a blazing beacon of light capable of dispelling the thick darkness that covers the nations. For all of his belief in it, Paul never tries to explain the resurrection of Jesus. He knows that to try to explain the ways of God in terms of human experience is like trying to explain the sun in terms of a candle. It is the sun that makes sense of the candle.

Likewise, we do not prove the resurrection. The resurrection proves us. Which is not to say that the Easter faith asks that we believe without proof, but rather that we trust without reservation.

These so-called "Jesus Wars" are being fought over a narrow, but important, piece of turf: What happened on Easter Day? Was the *body* of Jesus raised from the dead, or was it only the *Spirit* of Jesus? Proponents of the *bodily* resurrection claim that Jesus's tomb was empty because his body had been transformed into a new mode of physicality. Proponents of the *spiritual* resurrection of Jesus are skeptical about anything unusual having happened to Jesus's corpse. It is irrelevant to the truth of Easter—which is that the Spirit of the Living Christ still confronts us.

Sometimes, we need to be practical agnostics—there are things in the Christian faith we just do not know. Like one of my seminary professors put it, "Who of us was there?" Personally, I appreciate both perspectives. In the end, there is no final conflict between the "Jesus of History" and the "Christ of Faith."

The best, and I believe, the only adequate explanation for the rise of Christianity is the rising of Jesus. Those early Christians were convinced that Jesus was personally alive in and among them. They knew Jesus as their Lord in the power of the Spirit. Their lives and loves and values were changed. And from that they concluded that Israel's sin had been dealt with once and for all and God's new age had begun. It is unthinkable that Christianity would have continued if its advocates believed that their leader was dead.

The Christian religion is one of the most physical of all the world's great religions. Christians believe in "the resurrection of the body," not in "the immortality of the soul." God raised Jesus from the dead. God did not resuscitate his corpse from a clinical-death experience.

Further, the idea of the soul living on as a "disembodied spirit" is a pagan idea from Greek philosophy. It is neither Jewish nor Christian. First, it devalues the body by describing it as a tomb in which the soul is imprisoned. Second, it views death as a "liberation of the soul" to be welcomed, rather than "the last enemy to be destroyed" (as Paul put it in I Corinthians 15:26). Third, it makes Jesus's attitude toward his own death strange and incomprehensible. Why was his will to live so strong that he begged God with sweat and tears to "let this cup [of death] pass from me"? Jesus wanted to live! He did not want to die!

Whether you are a Thomas Jefferson, who cuts out of the Bible everything that sounds miraculous, including the resurrection, or you are a modern skeptic, who eliminates anything in the Bible that "offends modern rationality," or a logical positivist, who cannot believe what he or she cannot argue to deny or falsify, you cannot deny that something happened to those early followers of Jesus—something powerful enough to transform them from a cowardly band of disillusioned disciples hiding in fear into a mighty force that would change the course of world history. The only thing that could account for that phenomenal turnaround in their behavior is their unflinching proclamation that, "Jesus is Lord."

The question for us is not, "Was the resurrection real?" but, "Is the resurrection real for us?" Not, "Did it happen then, to them?" but, "Is it happening now, to us?" That means that Easter is more about humanity and the world being fully alive to the glory of God than it is about corpses disappearing or spirits floating around the earth.

"All appearances to the contrary, we no longer live in a Good Friday world. We live in an Easter world. The truth of Easter tells us that you can kill God's love, but you can never keep it dead and buried.

> *It says that all that strength and tenderness (and oh, how you*
> *have to be strong to be tender)...*
> *all that goodness that we say Friday scourged, buffeted, stretched*
> *out on a cross...*
> *that gorgeous life which continued to raise the strains of hope,*
> *even as they were being drowned out by orchestrated evil...*
> *that goodness in person on earth...*
> *is alive again,*
> *and 'Lo, I am with you always, to the end of the age.'"* [8]

"I am not suggesting that the resurrection is nonhistorical, but that the historical is the wrong category for understanding resurrection. The resurrection is not a fact to be believed, but an experience to be shared." [9]

On a global level, the death of Christ is the death of war. Either we put an end to war, or war will put an end to us. "It is time we stopped retreating from the giant social issues of the day into the pygmy world of private piety. The chief religious question is not, 'What must I do to be saved?' but rather, 'What must we all do to save God's creation?' . . . .

"Human unity is not something we are called on to create, only to recognize and make manifest. Territorial discrimination has always been as evil as racial, as Pablo Casals recognized when he asked: 'To love one's country is a splendid thing, but why should love stop at the border?'"[10]

If there are those who doubt the resurrection, let us put it to a proper, scientific test. The risen Christ told his disciples that he had been given "all authority in heaven and on earth," and that they were to, "Go and baptize the nations"—not individuals, nations. Let us bring that hypothesis into the laboratory of life.[11]

What would happen if those who have hurt each other—parents and children, husbands and wives, neighbors and friends, bosses and employees—made an attempt to see Christ in each other?

What would happen if Bill Clinton and Slobodan Milosevic had made and current world leaders would make an attempt to see in Christ's light millions of suffering and starving people in their own nations, deprived of the basics of life so that their resources can be used to build bombs and missiles?

What would happen if the family of Matthew Shepard and those who killed him so brutally because of his sexual orientation would see in each other's eyes the risen Christ?

What would happen if the abortion doctors with their bullet-proof vests and all the angry protesters with their placards of hate see in Christ the true definition of full humanity?

What would happen if the eight-year old girl in that third-world country, making running shoes for pennies a day and the share-holders of Nike met in each other's homes around a common meal?

What would happen if all of these opposing interests were to kneel in prayer on Easter? Then, as good scientists, we could observe the results. Such a test would be worthy of God's great faith in us, the faith which God demonstrated by sending Jesus into the world. Nothing less will prove the resurrection.

"Christ is risen 'pro nobis,' for us, to put love in our hearts, decent thoughts in our heads, and," as Bill Coffin put it, "a little more iron up our spines. Christ is risen to convert us, not from life to something more than life, but from something less than life to the possibility of full life itself. As it is written: The glory of God is a human being fully alive."[12]

Easter is the victory of seemingly powerless love over loveless power.

As Christians we may not know how Jesus got out of the tomb. But we do know that an empty tomb is nothing compared to the fact that we are forgiven. And that we are set free to be Christ's agents of change in a world of warring madness.

We may not know *what* is beyond the grave, but we do know *who* is beyond the grave. And there is more *mercy* in him than *sin* in us, more *love* in him than *fear* in us, more *light* in him than *darkness* in us, more *faith* in him than *doubt* in us, and *more hope for the world* in him than in anything else on the *horizon*.

> *"For as in Adam all die; so also,*
> *in Christ shall all be made alive."* (I Corinthians 15:22)

Because he lives, we shall live also.

> *"Thine is the Glory, Risen conquering Son;*
> *Endless is the victory Thou o'er death hast won."*[13]

CHAPTER 3

JESUS AS A
MOVEMENT INITIATOR

I submit that the history of the world consists of the descent of
fiery dreams to frozen memories. Every major social upheaval
begins with

    a MAN (OR WOMAN),

        turns into a MOVEMENT,

            is institutionalized in a MONUMENT,

                codified in a MANUAL,

                    and finally is entombed in a MUSEUM.

That is certainly true of Karl Marx and Communism and of
Nikolai Lenin and Socialism. It is true of Susan B. Anthony and
Women's Suffrage, of Mahatma Gandhi and Non-Violent
Resistance, and of Martin Luther King, Jr. and Anti-Racism.

And it is true of Jesus of Nazareth and Christianity. What began
as the flaming passion of a MAN on fire by God, became a revolutionary MOVEMENT within Judaism, which was soon institutionalized into a MONUMENT to Status-Quo Christianity, with a

MANUAL of Rules and Doctrines, and today is entombed in thousands of MUSEUMS throughout the Western world—opulent Gothic Cathedrals hosting thousands of tourists throughout the week, with but a meager handful of faithful worshippers on the Lord's Day.

If you and I are to encounter the original Jesus in any meaningful way at the end of the twenty-first century, we must experience him not only as a Jewish mystic, a wisdom teacher, a social prophet, and a healer, but also, if not primarily, as the Initiator of a Movement which went beyond reform and revolution to a world transformed.

Recently, the Episcopal Church in this country attempted to do this with the help of an advertising agency. In their print ads, Jesus looked curiously like Che Guevara, the 1960's radical. Needless to say, some traditional Episcopalians found this image somewhat of a cultural disconnect from the 1928 Book of Prayer! The ads were pulled immediately.

O.K., now to the point! Jesus brought into being a Jewish renewal movement that challenged and shattered the social, political, and economic boundaries of his day, a movement that eventually became institutionalized in the early Christian church and entombed in Western Christianity.

Jesus was media-savvy. He used dramatic public actions to make his point. "He ate meals with untouchables, which not only generated criticism but also symbolized his alternative vision of human community. He entered Jerusalem at the head of a procession on a donkey—a virtual parody of prevailing ideas of kingship. . . . He provocatively staged a demonstration in the temple, overturning the tables of the money changers and driving out the sellers of sacrificial animals."[14] That was an act of social protest tantamount to burning a flag or a draft card. A statement not as much against commerce and religion, but against the entire sacrificial religious system which excluded people from God, rather than inviting them into God's community.

"There was a radical social and political edge to [Jesus's] message and activity. He had a clever tongue, which could playfully or sarcastically indict the powerful and proper. He [was] remarkably courageous, willing to continue what he was doing even when it was clear that it was putting him in lethal danger."[15] As a result, while the founders of the world's other major religions lived long lives and were active for decades, Jesus lived only into his early thirties, and his public activity lasted as little as a year, and not more than three or four years.

Jesus's movement was not based in ideology or economics. It was based on compassion. For Jesus, compassion was the central quality of God and the central quality of a life centered in God. "Be compassionate as God is compassionate."[16] In the Gospel story in John, chapter 11, Jesus demonstrates this principle and "has compassion" on Lazarus and his family—not mere sentimental feelings with tears, but compassion which results in conviction and confrontation with the final enemy of life—death itself.

Although compassion was rooted in the Jewish tradition, it was not the dominant religious value. The primary value was holiness. It is in the conflict between these two qualities of God—holiness and compassion—that we see the central conflict in the ministry of Jesus: between two different social visions.

For Jesus, compassion was political. He was always in conflict with his critics about purity laws and issues. The purity system of Jesus's day applied to persons, places, things, times, and social groups. It created boundaries between pure and impure, acceptable and unacceptable, clean and unclean. Genetically, Israelites believed themselves to be pure. Converts were not as pure, illegitimates were further down the list, followed by those with damaged testicles, and then women.[17]

With regard to behavior, the religiously observant were "righteous," the tax collectors and shepherds were "outcasts" and "sinners." Those who ate pork and shellfish were impure. Those who did not were pure. The maimed, chronically ill, lepers, eunuchs, and so forth were impure. The abject poor were impure. Jews were more pure than Gentiles. And so on.

In the message and actions of Jesus, we see an alternative social vision: a community shaped not by the politics of purity, but by the politics of compassion. Jesus deliberately and radically replaced the core value of purity with compassion. True purity is not a matter of external boundaries and separation, but of the heart.

The inclusiveness of the Jesus movement continued into the early Christian community in the Book of Acts. The Ethiopian eunuch was sexually defective and impure by Jewish religious standards. But it meant nothing to Philip when he baptized him. Women were inferior to men in the purity codes. But it meant nothing to Paul when he declared, "In Christ there is neither . . . male nor female." The maimed and street beggars were unclean. But they were the first whom Jesus invited to share the intimacy of a common meal together with the wealthy and the physically attractive.

To encounter Jesus today has much to do with our presuppositions of clean and unclean. To encounter Jesus in a welfare line calls into question our assumption that "God blesses the righteous with wealth." To encounter Jesus in the dark-skinned face of an Arab calls into question our assumption that people who are different than we may not be as important. Likewise, to encounter Jesus in a multimillionaire, or in a White Anglo Saxon Protestant, calls into question our assumptions that others are less pure than we are because they are different than we are, and that our religious club is not for the likes of them.

Encountering Jesus means becoming part of the radical, revolutionary, alternative community of Jesus. Compassion is nonviolent.

Whenever we as a country finalize preparations for any military operations any place in the world, such as massive air strikes on Kosovo, we would do well to remember Jesus's caution not to return evil for evil. We become what we hate. "Whoever fights monsters," warned Friedrich Nietzsche, "should see to it that in the process he does not become a monster."

"You always become the thing you fight the most," wrote Carl Jung. The conflict in the Balkans was an illustration. As Miroslav Volf described it, "Once the conflict started, it seemed to trigger an uncontrollable chain reaction. These were decent people, helpful neighbors. They did not, strictly speaking, *choose* to plunder and burn, rape and torture—or secretly enjoy these. A dormant beast in them was awakened from its uneasy slumber."

And not only in them. The motives of those who set to fight against the brutal aggressors were self-defense and justice, but the beast in others enraged the beast in them. And so the moral barriers holding it in check were broken and the beast went after revenge. In resisting evil, people were trapped by it.[18]

The struggle against evil can make us evil if we use its methods. "The ultimate weakness of violence," said Martin Luther King, Jr., "is that it is a descending spiral, begetting the very thing it seeks to destroy."

"In a pluralistic world in which we are privileged to learn from all religious and philosophical traditions, Christians still have a story to tell to the nations. Who knows—telling it may do no one so much good as ourselves. And as we tell it and live it, we may see ourselves—and maybe even the world—a little bit transformed."[19]

The Christian religion began with a MAN aflame with the passion of a new society. If his MOVEMENT is to become more than a tourist's MUSEUM, we, his followers, must regain his passion. If not optimistic, we can be hopeful. If faith puts us on the road, hope is what keeps us there.

Hopeful people are always critical of the present, but only because they hold such a bright view of the future. Hope arouses in us a passion for the possible.

May it be so with us.

CHAPTER 4

JESUS AS A SOCIAL PROPHET

"To be born again is to see with even greater clarity the complexities of life and our own complicity in the very evils we abhor, and to dedicate ourselves as never before to the eradication of these evils—even if doing so results in our being 'lifted up,' as were the Son of man and many a disciple."[20]

Never would I have guessed that I would see that prediction come true for a dear friend. The Reverend Tom Otte, a fellow minister of the Presbytery of Southern New England, and a brother in Christ, was found murdered on March 4, 1999, in his Hartford home, just days after he had publicly identified himself as being gay. His body was stabbed and slashed beyond recognition. This was a brutal end for a very kind person.

Tom was an advocate for social justice and reconciliation. A Navy veteran and graduate of Princeton Theological Seminary, he was the staff chaplain at the Hartford Correctional Center and Hartford Hospital, a pastoral counselor, and had served for seven years as Parish Associate and Pastor of the First Presbyterian

Church, Holyoke, Massachusetts, until his resignation in 1998. He was a Commissioner from our Presbytery to the 209th General Assembly of the Presbyterian Church (U.S.A.) in 1997 and served with me and others on our Presbytery Council. His was a diverse, loving, active, and effective ministry as noted in one news report.

Tom was a "friend of Jesus" and a "friend of Jesus's friends." His ministry was with hurting people from all walks of life—prisoners, homeless men and women, refugees needing mentors, and especially with the ministry of Presbyterians for Gay and Lesbian Concerns, and with "More Light" churches, a national movement including Presbyterian churches, to welcome gays and lesbians into Christian congregations.

Tom and his wife Wilma's home was a "safe house" for all kinds of people. They never locked their doors to anyone. Nor did Tom after her death in 1997. Day or night, if you needed a friend, Tom was there for you. And it was that openness, that vulnerability, that Christ-like naiveté, that heart of love, that got him killed.

In 1998 Tom addressed the Presbytery of Southern New England. He spoke in solidarity with and on behalf of the scores of silenced men and women in our churches who have no voice, no vote, and no hope of ever being able to be true to their identity as God has created them. He admitted to having been scared over the years of speaking out so directly against the sin of heterosexism and the exclusion of his friends from our Presbyterian churches. He pleaded for a reversal of our silent exclusivity, and his voice faltered when he begged us to watch out for attacks of the opposition sneaking up on us from behind.

After the vote that day against Amendment "B," which prohibits the ordination of those who are not faithful in marriage or celibate in singleness from being ordained as pastors, elders, or deacons in the Presbyterian Church (U.S.A.), Tom told me privately that he would not have had the courage to speak out as he did had that Assembly meeting not been held at my progressive church in New Canaan. He said, "Gary, I thank God for you and your church. This is a safe place in an unsafe denomination."

After Tom's death, one of our members wrote this tribute:

"He was a sanctuary for those who were rejected by a society at large, a listening post, a lighthouse in a tempestuous sea, a rock that the discarded and disfavored and outcast could rely upon in time of need. His work may not have conformed to the standards set by his community, or even accepted by the community at large, but this is where he left his imprint, his mark, by offering a refuge for those who were shunned by the very society that enveloped him. All of this should sound very familiar if one turns the pages of history back some 2,000 years."[21]

And so it does. Jesus was not only a Jewish mystic and a wisdom teacher. He was a social prophet. He was a "God-intoxicated" advocate of social justice. Like other prophets of ancient Israel, his authority and social passion came from the immediacy of his experience of God and not from institutional authorization. As the prophet Amos proclaimed:

> *"The Lord roars from Zion . . .*
> *The lion has roared . . .*
> *The Lord God has spoken, who can but prophesy?*
> *The Lord took me from following the flock,*
> *and said to me, "Go, prophesy to my people Israel."*[22]

Those who know the immediacy of God are typically on the side of the marginalized. This was particularly true of the sharp social boundaries of the "purity laws" of Jesus's day. For Jesus and his opponents, purity was not a matter of piety but of politics.[23]

As my wife Bev puts it so colorfully, "Jesus ate and drank with the hoi polloi, the Roman tax collectors, and the ladies of the local Escort Club." He treated children as children and not as misshapen little adults. He spoke out against the "moral majority" of his day and called them "whited sepulchers." He wept over Lazarus and Jerusalem, which "real men" don't do. He intentionally worked at healing on the sacred Sabbath. He spoke openly with women in public, and he took away the stigma of "unclean" from the poor, from social outcasts and racial half-breeds.

Consider the story about the woman from Samaria recounted in John 4:

> *She was the wrong race—a hybrid despised by both Jews and Gentiles.*
>
> *She was the wrong sex—women of her day were spit on by men and treated as second-class baggage.*
>
> *She was the wrong partner—she had been used and abused by five husbands, each of whom had divorced her when he was finished with her.*
>
> *She was the wrong age—men wanted only young girls as wives in those days. (Some things never change!)*
>
> *She was in the wrong profession—only slaves and household servants did her kind of work.*
>
> *She was likely an outcast in her own village—why else would she make that long journey at 12 noon to draw water from the well, in the blazing heat of the day, unless she was trying to avoid public shame?*

She was, in fact, a symbol of all that is beautiful, vulnerable, and holy, having been ground into the dry desert dirt under the heel of pathetic, scared, needy little men who could only define themselves over and against women. And so the men gathered together daily to bond with others like themselves and pray the ancient prayer: "Lord, I thank Thee that I was not born a woman."

There is no gender-based appropriateness to vulnerability. Vulnerability is not a feminine trait. It is a human trait. As St. Paul put it, "Whenever I am weak, then I am strong."[24] "Without it there can be neither honesty nor intimacy. Without vulnerability we don't really meet one another, we just bump masks."[25]

The more we open ourselves to Divine Love, the less we have to fear. God's love is visionary. It doesn't seek value, it creates it.

With Marcus Borg, I am convinced that it was primarily Jesus's activity as a social prophet that accounted for his execution. The world cannot tolerate pure love. Jesus died because he loved too much, with a tough love that dared to challenge our prejudices. Tom Otte died from that same love.

Let us take courage that the 1999 final decision of the Permanent Judicial Commission of our Presbytery regarding the trial of the Stamford Church Session's desire to install a gay elder who is "in a loving relationship." The Associated Press reported that the Commission decided by a vote of four to one in favor of the Stamford session. My friend and Elder Wayne Osborne can return to his work in leading that church.

Tragically, Tom Otte did not live long enough to see this day. But we would not have seen it were it not for him, and scores of prophets like him, who have been "lifted up," even as was our Lord Jesus.

If a lamp went out, it was because for Tom, at least, the Dawn had come. So let us not give up, but seek consolation in that love which never dies, and find our hope in that redeeming love that always is.

Thanks be to God for his redeeming love. May it empower us to do his work.

CHAPTER 5

JESUS AS A WISDOM TEACHER

Mark Twain once observed, "The cat, having sat upon a hot stove lid, will not sit upon a hot stove lid again. Nor upon a cold stove lid. Once burned, twice foolish."

Most of us live our lives by this kind of wisdom, even when it contradicts itself. In his delightful book, *Maybe (Maybe Not)*, Robert Fulghum calls attention to the contradictions of proverbial wisdom. Consider these examples:

> *Look before you leap.*
> *He who hesitates is lost.*
>
> *Two heads are better than one.*
> *If you want something done right, do it yourself.*
>
> *Nothing ventured, nothing gained.*
> *Better safe than sorry.*

You can't teach an old dog new tricks.
It's never too late to learn.

Never sweat the small stuff.
God is in the details.[26]

If these pieces of advice seem conflicting, contradictory, or paradoxical, it is because human existence is conflicting, contradictory, and paradoxical. Life is ambiguous. Try as we might, we can never make it all fit. We do not live in an ordered universe that ultimately makes sense of our intellectual and moral experience.

This is not good news for people who think they "have it all together." "Knowledge is proud that he has learned so much; wisdom is humble that he does not know more." (William Cowper)

Such is the so-called wisdom of those who gave us Amendment "B" in our Presbyterian Constitution. Requiring officers of the church to "repent of all things the Book of Confessions calls 'sins,'" in order to be acceptable to God and the church is hardly clear thinking. At the time papers reported that a large number of elders in the First Presbyterian Church of Stamford admitted that they were unrepentant about some of their behavior which church law deems sins: like, playing the lottery, watching football on the Sabbath, and keeping pictures or statues of Jesus in their homes.

True! If we went by the book, we would be requiring our officers to repent, not just of unfaithfulness and unchasteness, or having lusted in their hearts, but of having married divorced persons, having prayed to a Saint, having not tithed ten percent, having not kept a kosher kitchen, having complained about paying taxes, having used deceptive advertising, having been drunk, gluttonous, greedy, idle, envious, having enhanced the price of a commodity, having farmed to the edge of their fields, having worn a fabric woven with more than one kind of thread, or having ever eaten lobster or barbecued spare ribs. To name only a few "sins" listed in the Scriptures and Confessions.[27]

And of course, under Amendment "B," if you are gay or lesbian, you must repent of any attempt to live your life in an ordered, shared, monogamous, lifelong committed partnership with another person—which is why the Stamford Church session was up on charges.

That is why the Session of my church, the First Presbyterian Church of New Canaan, went on record as opposing Amendment "B" and determined to work for its removal from the Presbyterian Constitution.

Over 75 years ago, Harry Emerson Fosdick proclaimed, "If we are to reach a happy solution to this problem, [we need] a clear insight into the main issues of [contemporary] Christianity and a sense of penitent shame that the Christian church should be quarreling over little matters when the world is dying of great needs. . . . The Christian churches are making of themselves a cockpit of controversy when there is not a single thing at stake in the controversy on which depends the salvation of human souls. That is the trouble with this whole business. So much of it does not matter! What does matter—more than anything else in all the world— is that men and women in their personal lives and in their social relationships should know Jesus Christ."[28]

Let's be clear. Unity in the church is not based on agreement, but on mutual concerns. The problem, as many of us see it, is not illegal behavior; it is legalism. The problem is not unreligious passion; it is uncompassionate religion. The problem is not homosexuality; it is heterosexism.

Most of us are uncomfortable with constant change. Human beings have a general intolerance for non-conforming ideas. We tend to hold certainty dearer than truth. We want to know what we already know. We want to become what we already are. In psychological terms, we want to be more effective neurotics, "preferring the security of known misery to the misery of unfamiliar insecurity."[29]

The result is a kind of belief that makes us smaller rather than larger: A belief system that walls us inside rather than bridging us to others. A kind of legalism that makes authority our truth rather than truth our authority. A non-Christian orthodoxy that prefers the purity of dogma to the purity of love. This kind of knowledge prefers certainty to truth. It loves answers and hates questions. It loves absolutism and hates ambiguity. Worst of all, this kind of false wisdom demands premature closure—it cannot survive in the tension between two or more perspectives.

"The original confessions of faith," notes the distinguished Swiss theologian Hans Kung, "were in no way concerned with dogmas in the present-day sense. They were not doctrinal laws." Far from representing "a legal foundation," the early confessions were "a free expression of the faith of the community." But all that changed as the concept of orthodoxy began to take hold. And with orthodoxy came heresy.

Bruce Bawer, in his book, *Stealing Jesus: How Fundamentalism Betrays Christianity*, calls this increasing division in Christianity "The Church of Law" versus "The Church of Love." Tragically, religion in America is becoming a Church of Law. I submit that any church must be a Church of Love if it is true to the calling of Jesus.

Jesus undermined the world of conventional wisdom. He turned it on its head. He spoke of impossible combinations: "good Samaritans," "blessed poor," "the great Kingdom of God the size of a mustard seed," something impure, for children, outcasts, undesirables, nobodies—a Kingdom which is not somewhere else, but among us, inside us, and outside us, not just "then and there," but "here and now."

Jesus never preached religion. He was never content to parrot old proverbs. He knew that life was not a true/false test of knowing the right answers and keeping the rules, but a God-given challenge to color outside of the lines of traditional boundaries. Jesus was not content until he illuminated life and created fresh possibilities and with them, fresh difficulties with which to grapple.

Nicodemus would likely have preferred to remain ignorant than to have had his religious world view shattered by Jesus. He represented the power and tradition of the nation. He was the confident spokesperson of a fixed, immutable world, in which nothing ever changes. "Nicodemus represents that arrogant, orderly part of us and our world coolly confident about human knowledge and cynically sure of what is possible and impossible. Jesus, on the other hand, enfleshes the unpredictable reality of God and the world and the free breezes of the Spirit."[30]

"Rabbi, we know," began Nicodemus. "No, you don't know," countered Jesus. "Don't be astonished that I said to you, 'You must be born from above.' The wind of God's Spirit blows where it chooses, and it is beyond your knowing."

The Way of Jesus invites us to move from conventional wisdom, which is "secondhand religion," to subversive wisdom, which is "firsthand religion." To be "born again," or better, "born from above," has to do with living in and by the Spirit of God rather than in and by our airtight beliefs about God.

"To be born again is to see with even greater clarity the complexities of life and our own complicity in the very evils we abhor, and to dedicate ourselves as never before to the eradication of these evils—even if doing so results in our being 'lifted up,' as were the Son of man and many a disciple."[31]

As Bill Coffin often said and I often quote, "Christians believe in the Word made flesh, not in the Word made words." Christianity is less a set of beliefs than it is a way of life. The integrity of love is more important than the purity of dogma. I think we know far more of God's heart than we do of God's mind. "God is love, and those who abide in love abide in God and God abides in them."

For the Christian, wisdom is not advice, no matter how good it might be. And it is not law, no matter how just it is. Wisdom is a person, who brings to birth in each of us the subversive, earth shattering heartbeat of love.

Instead of, "Once burned, twice foolish," how about, "Once loved, twice loving"?

DIVERSITY
OF THOUGHT
FOR THE
PROGRESSIVE
CHRISTIAN

CHAPTER 6

RECOGNIZE THE FAITHFULNESS OF OTHER PEOPLE

*"Beloved, let us love one another, for love is from God;
everyone who loves is born of God and knows God."*
—I JOHN 4:7

In 2006 Americans awoke to news from Baghdad that the nation of Iraq was standing on the precipice of a catastrophic civil war. Unrestrained violence had broken out on all fronts: the insurgent bombing of a major Shiite shrine by Sunnis Arabs followed by a wave of killings of Sunnis by marauding gangs and by members of the Iraqi Army and the police.

Even as some Shiite and Sunni Muslim clerics were preaching against the rioting, each was blaming the other for the violence and both were hostile to the American role in Iraq. "Everybody seems to be imprisoned in their own sectarian or political affiliations," said the former Iraqi Foreign Minister. "They don't seem to be able to rise above these things."[32]

As Americans, we knew well what would happen if all efforts proved incapable of stopping an all-out civil war. As Abraham Lincoln said of our own nation's greatest ordeal, "All dreaded it ... all sought to avert it . . . and the war came."

Intolerance of diversity, especially religious diversity, is not just a Middle East phenomenon. Here is what some of our American clergy preached:

On the 700 Club, Reverend Pat Robertson told thousands of his followers:
> *"You say you're supposed to be nice to the Episcopalians and the Presbyterians and the Methodists and this, that, and the other thing. Nonsense. I don't have to be nice to the spirit of the Antichrist."*

And again from the same preacher,
> *"(T)he feminist agenda is not about equal rights for women. It is about a socialist, anti-family political movement that encourages women to leave their husbands, kill their children, practice witchcraft, destroy capitalism and become lesbians."*

Speaking about the September 11 terrorist attacks, Reverend Jerry Falwell said,
> *"I really believe that the pagans, and the abortionists, and the feminists, and the gays and lesbians who are actively trying to make that an alternative lifestyle . . . I point the finger in their face and say 'you helped this happen.'"*

And again,
> *"I [We] will not adopt 'inclusive' policies to accept other religious teachings."*[33]

Christian activist Randall Terry proclaimed:
> *"Our goal [for America] is a Christian nation. We have a*

Biblical duty; we are called by God to conquer this country. We don't want equal time. We don't want pluralism. We want theocracy. Theocracy means God rules . . .

"I want you to just let a wave of intolerance wash over you. I want you to let a wave of hatred wash over you. Yes, hate is good. . . When I, or people like me, are running the country, you'd better flee, because we will find you, we will try you, and we will execute you."[34]

In times of fear and panic, people gravitate to simple solutions for complex problems. But "thinking Christians" learn to live with ambiguity. Many Christians prefer certainty to truth. Yet Christ promises us risk, not certainty. That is what Progressive Christians believe and try to practice. Theirs are churches where all people are welcome, where a variety of paths toward compassion, inclusion, and God are honored, and where the only heresy lies in pretending that there is only one way and that God is on that side.

Progressive Christians try to have an expansive, not a restrictive, vision of the world. They try not to be fearful of "the other." They believe that sincere differences beautify the pattern, and that the whole human sound goes up to God in praise only from the full orchestra of humanity. As the second point of the Statement of Progressive Christianity puts it, "We are Christians who recognize the faithfulness of other people who have other names for their ways into God's realm, and we acknowledge that their ways are true for them, as our ways are true for us."

Progressive Christians find our approach to God through Jesus Christ. But we do not believe we have a better access to God than do other people—or that our way is right and theirs is wrong. For us, Jesus is the essential definition of God. In his life and teachings, we see clearly what a life full of God, a life full of Love, looks like. For us, Jesus is the definition of what it means to be truly human as well as truly divine. We see in him the type of person all of us were created to be.

For Christians, Jesus is "the Way, the Truth, and the Life." We are convinced Christians who are attempting to make sense of our lives within the Christian framework and tradition. But we would never say to another person, "We welcome everyone as long as you are willing to become like us . . ." or, "We accept you just as you are . . . now change!" To do that would be to reduce God to our understanding of God. And God is always bigger than any of our ideas about God.

Case-in-point is the amazing inclusiveness of the Hebrew prophet Micah, telling a nation of committed Jews that not just Judaism, but that each of our varied religions may well co-exist for all time: "All people will walk, each in the names of their Gods, and we will walk in the name of the Lord our God for ever and ever!"

But, then, what do we do with that Bible verse in John 14:6 which has Jesus saying, "I am the way, the truth and the life; no one comes to God (or 'the father') but by me"?

First of all, we must remember that the Gospel of John was not written until some 100 years after Jesus's birth by a young, enthusiastic group of Jews who disagreed with each other about letting gentiles into their group. What you had in that early congregation was the younger "Jews for Jesus" fighting with the older "Jews for the Bible" over the question of who could be admitted into their new community. "The fourth Gospel is not concerned with the fate, for example, of Muslims, Hindus, or Buddhists, nor with the superiority or inferiority of Judaism and Christianity. . . ."[35]

What we see in John 14 is an inter-Nicene conflict within the early church. Just four verses after this seeming exclusionary verse, Jesus is quoted as saying, "In my father's house are many dwelling places. . . "[36] What that text most likely meant was that there was plenty of room in God's house for all kinds of people, not just Christians!

There are a number of other ways to think about this as well. It is quite possible, for instance, to be a "Christian Universalist," which is to believe that the life and death of Christ changed the world. As St. Paul puts it, "God was in Christ reconciling the world to Godself" (not just Christians). And, as he wrote to Timothy, "Christ is the savior of all, especially those who believe."[37]

The problem some of us have with that position is that it infers that every person on earth, regardless of their religion, is in fact, an "Anonymous Christian" who just doesn't know they are! That is hardly the best way to celebrate diversity! That is somewhat akin to someone telling me that I am an "Anonymous Hindu," although I do gladly admit to having being told I am a "Secret Rabbi"!

The important thing to remember is that no one has ever been saved by doctrine or religious dogma. Damned, yes. But saved, no.

Neither philosophy nor theology nor religion can save us. As St. Augustine put it, "Theology is faith in search of understanding." At best, good theology can provide a framework to help us make some sense of our lives and our faith. But in the end, our salvation is not in our belief in God, but in God's belief in us.

Our responsibility is not to try to convert others from the grounding of their spiritual anchors. Our responsibility is to listen with genuine respect and with anticipation that we have much to learn from them. With that in mind, it is also our responsibility to share with them what we have experienced in Jesus Christ . . . a presence of the spirit of God who loves the world and all its people, and who is at work to bring to completion throughout the entire creation a vision of love, hope, justice, peace, and fulfillment.

"Being, life and love transcend all boundaries. No sacred scripture of any religious tradition can any longer claim that in its pages the fullness of God has been captured."[38]

Rather, as Krister Stendahl suggests, we must learn to like the others in their otherness. "We might even indulge in a bit of 'holy envy,'" he says. "That is, we might see something beautiful in what is different from us, something highly desirable, instead of trying to find ways in which we are the same."[39] We need religious diversity in order to realize our full potential as human beings.

When that happens, "A new day will be born, and Jesus – who

crossed every boundary of tribe, prejudice, gender and religion—will be honored by those of us who, as his disciples, have transcended the boundaries of even the religious system that was created to honor him."[40]

As the fourth point of Progressive Christianity affirms, we "invite all people to participate in our community and worship life without insisting that they become like us in order to be acceptable (including but not limited to): believers and agnostics, conventional Christians and questioning skeptics, women and men, those of all sexual orientations and gender identities, those of all races and cultures, those of all classes and abilities, those who hope for a better world and those who have lost hope."[41]

Many Christians today are amused by stories about nineteenth century missionaries who insisted that their converts around the Pacific Rim dress in the European fashion and sing western tunes accompanied by portable organs. Yet some of those same Christians, who claim to welcome all people, expect their new members eventually to look like themselves. They assume that doubters and skeptics will become believers, that gays and lesbians will become straight, that everyone will appear to be cheerful.

Progressive Christians take a different approach. From our reading of the gospels, we have come to the conclusion that the followers of Jesus are to welcome all people without imposing on them the necessity of changing their culture, their understanding of faith, their politics, their economics, or their particular orientation. To take this position a step farther, we would also say that the established members of a church should always be alert to the possibility that they are the ones who must do the changing.

"Today, 'everyone is the next-door neighbor and spiritual neighbor of everyone else in the world,' as the Catholic theologian Karl Rahner put it. Neighborliness means that absolute claims for oneself and one's beliefs are necessarily mitigated by an absolute respect for the rights of others to hold very different beliefs."[42]

My final point to make here is that, as Progressive Christians, "we find more grace in the search for understanding than we do in dogmatic certainty—more value in questioning than in absolutes."[43]

We are accustomed to thinking of church as a source of security and comfort, if not complete certainty. Sometimes the conflict and confusion that arise from thoughtful faith can be scary.

Jim Adams, one of the founders of The Center for Progressive Christianity, puts his finger on the cause of this. "When people really come up close to contradiction, I think it's the fear of the Infinite." Yet, he says, "I think it is in the midst of that tension that we're closest to God. So the fear is natural and appropriate. One way to deal with fear is to cling tenaciously to one pole or the other. Whereas for me, faithfulness is moving forward in spite of the fear."[44]

Let me be clear about this: God is not found in our doctrinal distinctive nor our creedal confession nor our theological dogmatism nor our liturgical practice nor in our denominational distinctiveness. God is found in our relationship with the universe, the spiritual life, and one another, not in our dogma.

"God is love, and those who abide in love abide in God and God abides in them."

May it eventually be so here in every town in America and in every country throughout the world.

CHAPTER 7

CREATION NON-SCIENCE

The day will come when, after harnessing space, the winds,
the tides and gravitation, we shall harness for God the energies of love.
And on that day, for the second time in the history of the world,
we shall have discovered fire.
—Pierre Teilhard de Chardin

There is a story about a group of scientists, and they were all sitting around discussing which one of them was going to go to God and tell him that they didn't need him anymore. Finally, one of the scientists volunteered and went to go tell God that he was no longer needed.

So the scientist says to God, "God, you know a bunch of us have been thinking, and I've come to tell you that we really don't need you anymore. I mean, we've been coming up with great theories and ideas, we've cloned sheep, and we're on the verge of cloning humans. So as you can see, we really don't need you."

God nods understandingly and says: "I see. Well, no hard feelings. But before you go, let's have a contest. What d'ya think?"

The scientist says: "Sure, I'm all for it. What kind of contest?"

God replies, "A man-making contest."

The scientist says, "Sure! No problem." The scientist bends down and picks up a handful of dirt and says: "Okay, I'm ready!"

And God says, "No, no. You go get your own dirt!"

End of contest!

For many Christians, the creation of the world is a divine miracle, but not a human mystery. Their strong conviction is that God created the world and all that is in it in six 24-hour days, and then rested on the seventh when his work was done. When you ask them, "How do you know this for sure?" they declare confidently, "Because the Bible says so. God said it, Moses wrote it, and I believe it. End of story."

Two thousand years ago the Apostle Paul exclaimed, "O the depth of the riches both of the wisdom and knowledge of God! How unsearchable are God's judgments and God's ways past finding out! For who has known the mind of God?"[45]

Yet today, half of the Christians in America believe that they know exactly how the world was created because God told them so in the Bible—and every word in that Book is factual and without error because God dictated every letter of it. Personally, I cannot believe in a God like that who would write a book like that. A God who did his best work in creating human beings is highly unlikely to require them to check their minds at the door of the sanctuary or when they read the Bible. The Bible is the inspired Word of God, passionate stories of the human search for God written by people like you and me, with all of our limitations, and culturally conditioned by our place in history.

Frankly, I think we know far more of God's heart than we do of God's mind. God's "revelation is in the relationship. And a relationship with God provides more psychological certitude than intellectual certainty. Faith is not believing without proof; it is trusting without reservation. . . . We do not sharpen our minds by narrowing them."[46]

As Rabbi Balfour Brickner said, "The Bible is the most dangerous book in the world. . . . A simple reading of the first eleven chapters of Genesis can make an agnostic, if not an atheist, out of anyone who has ever taken an introductory course in biology, physics, astronomy, or for that matter, the history of the Middle East. . . . [These chapters] are myths that may—and I do believe do—reveal good moral and ethical truths, but not factual truths."[47]

In 1611 the King James translation of the Bible was published with a note to readers that the Creation of the World had occurred on the evening before the 23rd of October in the year 4004 B.C. That same dating is noted in the Scofield Reference Bible used by thousands of Christians today.

In 1616 the Roman Catholic Church banned all books that suggested the earth was not the center of the universe (and presumably the center of God's attention, as well). In 1632 the astronomer Galileo was ordered to appear before the Church's Inquisition. In his defense, he argued that the Bible was never intended to be a scientific document. "The Bible tells us how to go to heaven," he said, "not how the heavens go." Galileo spent the last eight years of his life under house arrest in his villa outside of Florence. "While his daughter read him the seven daily psalms of penitence that were a part of his sentence, the old man sat by the window where he could watch the planets through his telescope."[48]

Surveys over the past few years are equally discouraging. 40% of Americans favor teaching what is called "creation science" instead of evolution in our public schools. They demand that the Bible become the classroom textbook. Fully 68% would like to see creationism given equal time with cosmic and biological evolution. What a distorted view of both science and the Bible. Genesis 1 "no more belongs in a high school science textbook than pages of that textbook would belong in the hymn books of the church," as Martin Marty puts it.

A student once reportedly asked St. Augustine what God was doing BEFORE creating the heavens and the earth. The theologian was speechless for a moment, and then replied, "Creating Hell, for snips like you who ask me questions like that!"

What is happening, it seems, is that the older religious view (i.e., literal Biblical creation) is being replaced by a newer secular view (i.e., a scientific, mechanistic universe). But neither of these is satisfactory. There is ample room within a progressive view of the Bible, God, and the world to accommodate the best of science alongside the best of theology. Theology is not science nor should it be. Theology at its best is still "faith seeking understanding." Science may discover the mechanism of the universe. But only faith can discover its meaning.

The problem is that everyone assumes the limits of his or her own perspective to be limits of the world. The poet, Simon Parke, acknowledges this in his poem, "Question Time":

> *"The scientist asks how it works.*
> *The painter asks how it looks.*
> *The counselor asks how it feels.*
> *The mystic asks where it came from.*
> *And they all need each other."*[49]

As Annie Dillard put it in her book, *Teaching a Stone to Talk*: "The question from agnosticism is, 'Who turned on the lights?' The question from faith is, 'Whatever for?'"

I have been inspired over the years by reading how our U.S. astronauts have spoken about their spiritual experiences in space. John Glenn, in his broadcast from the Discovery Space Shuttle on November 1, 1998, said to the nation, "I don't think you can be up here and look out the window as I did the first day and see the Earth from this vantage point, to look out at this kind of creation and not believe in God. To me, it's impossible—it just strengthens my faith. I wish there were words to describe what it's like . . . truly awesome."

James Irwin, another astronaut, wrote, "The Earth reminded us of a Christmas tree ornament hanging in the blackness of space. As we got farther and farther away it diminished in size. Finally it shrank to the size of a marble, the most beautiful marble you can imagine. That beautiful, warm, living object looked so fragile, so delicate, that if you touched it with a finger it would crumble and fall apart. Seeing this has to change a man, has to make a man appreciate the creation of God and the love of God."

Edgar Mitchell, yet another astronaut, said, "Instead of an intellectual search, there was suddenly very deep gut feeling that something was different . . . that there was a purposefulness of flow, of energy, of time, of space in the cosmos . . . that suddenly there was a nonrational way of understanding. . . . On the return trip home, gazing through 24,000 miles of space, I suddenly experienced the universe as intelligent, loving, harmonious."

Those kinds of testimonials help one understand why Alan Shepard looked back at Earth from the window of his space shuttle and wept.

No less a stellar light than Albert Einstein said, "My religion consists of a humble admiration of the illimitable superior spirit who reveals himself in the slight details we are able to perceive with our frail and feeble minds. That deeply emotional conviction of the presence of a superior reasoning power, which is revealed in the incomprehensible universe, forms my idea of God."[50]

Faith is not the opposite of science; it is its complement. In *The Brothers Karamazov*, Elder Zosima explains, "Each time you pray, if you do so sincerely, there will be a flash of a new feeling in it, and a new thought as well . . . one that will give you courage and you will understand that prayer is education. . . . [So] love all God's creation, both the whole of it and every grain of sand. Love every leaf, every ray of God's light. Love animals, love plants, love each thing. If you love each thing, you will perceive the mystery of God in all things. Once you perceive it, you will begin tirelessly to perceive more and more of it every day."

This all sums up my theology of creation, one of the great controversies over time that has created great divides between groups of Christians, as well as between Christians and other believers, and between Christians and members of the non-believing secular community. This is just another of those intellectual areas where we must accept our diversity and agree to disagree.

I pray every day that, as Pierre Teilhard de Chardin prayed, "The day will come when, after harnessing space, the winds, the tides, and gravitation, we shall harness for God the energies of love. And on that say, for the second time in the history of the world, we shall have discovered fire!"

CHAPTER 8

INVITE ALL PEOPLE TO PARTICIPATE

*"We walk in our religious paths toward the truth that is God.
But we do not possess it."*
—JOHN SHELBY SPONG

*"Whatever we do here will be to the right of Jesus,
who is to the right of God."*
—MARCUS BORG

*"Jesus Christ was not God's entry into human life. . . . It was this
divine involvement in human history, hidden from the beginning . . .
that was made manifest in Jesus. . . . In Christ is revealed that the
way of God's presence is incarnation. God acts through the human
in ordinary words and gestures, in impersonal relations."*
—GREGORY BAUM

"The true paradigm of the ordinary American view of Jesus is
Superman: 'Faster than a speeding bullet, more powerful than a
locomotive, able to leap tall buildings in a single bound. It's

Superman! Strange visitor from another planet, who came to earth with powers and abilities far beyond those of mortal men, and who, disguised as Clark Kent, mild-mannered reporter for a great metropolitan newspaper, fights a never ending battle for truth, justice and the American Way.' If that isn't popular Christology, I'll eat my hat. Jesus—gentle, meek and mild, but with secret, souped-up, more-than-human insides—bumbles around for thirty-three years, nearly gets himself done in for good by the Kryptonite Kross, but at the last minute, struggles into the phone booth of the Empty Tomb, changes into his Easter suit and with a single bound, leaps back up to the planet Heaven. It's got it all—including, just so you shouldn't miss the lesson, kiddies: *He never once touches Lois Lane.*"[51]

"No historical figure has generated more commentary and controversy than Jesus of Nazareth. Such attention is extraordinary in light of the fact that his career lasted at most only a few years and his activities were confined to his own homeland and ethnic group. Yet, the brief life and narrowly focused ministry of this first century Palestinian Jew became the basis for what is now a religion of universal appeal with the largest number of followers in the world. . . .

"One of the many things that have made Jesus so intriguing and the subject of so much discussion and debate is that he was and is such a man of mystery—a person who is rarely visible, and only in soft focus. He left no writings, apparently spoke and taught in an oblique and ambiguous style that puzzled even his closest followers, and—despite later claims to the contrary—founded no institution and left no clear agenda or program to be followed in his name. Complicating the situation is the fact that most of what we know about Jesus is based on New Testament writings that were composed long after the fact, are very sketchy and often contradictory, and are already biased by several layers of Christian belief, interpretation, and intent. . . .

"It is no wonder, then, that successive generations have remembered this man in a variety of ways, refashioning him time and again in their own images. He has been portrayed as everything from a simple rabbi to a deluded religious fanatic to a revolutionary zealot to the redeemer of all humanity. He has been reconceived in every culture and age according to its own standards and values, hopes and aspirations, and by countless individuals in light of their own predispositions, preferences, and prejudices. Historians of Christianity and Christian thought have shown again and again how views of and beliefs about Jesus have grown, developed, changed, and been codified (and sometimes condemned) in doctrines and dogmas over the centuries."[52]

A major re-visioning of Christianity is underway today, especially in the United States. When I use the term, "re-visioning," what I mean to describe is a faithful attempt on the part of many to "re-vision," to attempt "to see again" the meanings of Jesus for our life and faith together.

My main point is that Christianity is not a matter of *believing* the right things about God and Jesus, but about *living in relationship* with the Living Christ within the sacramental community of faith. In other words, faith is not a *noun*, it is a *verb*.

The Bible and the Christian tradition are mediators of the sacred. They do not fully reveal God to us, but rather point us in the direction of God. We are not meant to believe in them, but rather to believe in that to which they point. In this way they are like fingers pointing to The Way. "Believing in Jesus does not mean believing doctrines about him," as Marcus Borg puts it. "Rather, it means to give one's heart, one's self at it deepest level, to . . . the living Lord."

The unique affirmation of Christianity is that, unlike any other of the world's major religions, we find the revelation of God to us primarily in a *person*, not in a creed or a sacred writing. In Judaism and Islam, Moses and Muhammad are receivers of revelation, but God is not revealed in them fully as persons. Rather, God is revealed in the teachings of the Torah and the Qur'an. So it is in Buddhism: the revelation of God is not the Buddha as a person, but rather the Buddha's teachings that disclose the path to enlightenment and compassion. This does not make Christianity superior to other religions, but it does make it unique.[53]

The Christian tradition speaks of Jesus as 'fully God and fully man.' What does this mean? I like the way Marcus Borg puts it: "This is the central meaning of incarnation: Jesus is what can be seen of God embodied in a human life. He is the revelation, the incarnation, of God's character and passion—of what God is like and of what God is most passionate about. He shows us the heart of God. . . . Jesus is more central than the Bible; when they disagree, Jesus wins."[54]

In Jesus "the Word became flesh and lived among us, full of grace and truth." This high statement of Jesus's full humanity and full divinity, written by the author of the Gospel of John at the end of the first century, did not take its present form until 400 years after Jesus's death and resurrection. Our religion's orthodox Christological formula was finally produced by the Council of Chalcedon in 451 AD. The person of Jesus the Christ was said to be both fully God and fully human, two complete natures seamlessly fused—yet absolutely unmixed—in one unique person.

But that was not what Jesus's followers thought of him. It evolved over hundreds of years from three other master images. First there was the *"The Historical Jesus."* This is what we think might be the actual life and doings of Jesus (reported in Mark's Gospel) from the beginning sayings of his public ministry around 29 CE, until his death just a few years later. This image was followed by *"The Narrative Jesus."* These are the teachings, attitudes, deeds, and life drama of Jesus expressed in the stories of Jesus told by his early followers, mostly recorded in Matthew and Luke, around 70-85 CE. Finally there was *"The Sacred Christ,"* intimations of Jesus's divinity mostly from the high Christology of Paul, around 50 CE, and John, around 100 CE.

Thinking about how these various images of Jesus came to be is important not only because it helps us remember that Jesus was many things to many people, but also because it reminds us that he continues to be that for people today. Those who tend to value the *intellect and reason*, for example, take a great deal of interest in the Historical Jesus. The *ethically-oriented* tend to concentrate more on the moral teachings of the Historical or the Narrative Jesus (or both). The *devotionally-focused* Christian would tend to gravitate toward John's Sacred Christ. While the *mystical believer* would focus primarily on the Archetypal Christ of the Chalcedonian formulation. (Paul Laughlin)

Christians claim that something happens to us when we follow Jesus and we see him in everyone we meet, just as something happened to the followers of Jesus in his own day. What did they see in Jesus?

New Testament scholar Walter Wink puts it this way: They saw a human being fully alive, and for them, such life carried divine power and authority. But more important, this way of being fully and freely human "had now entered the heart of reality as a catalyst in human transformation. Like a bell that reverberates to the core of our being [Jesus, the incarnate Word of God], the [one, fully] Human Being is, as it were, an invitation to become the fullness of who we are. And with the invitation comes the power to do it."[55]

Personally speaking, Jesus is the *heart* of my faith. In Jesus, God speaks God's word to me. God's spirit becomes incarnate—"enfleshed"—in my flesh and blood. In him, all of life is sacred. "Jesus laughed, wept, scolded, reasoned, argued, cajoled, loved deeply, suffered disappointment, studied, worshiped, prayed intensely, faced despair, celebrated, stayed up late at night, ate, drank, partied, and healed people." (Gilbert Friend-Jones)

Fred Plumer puts it this way: "'You want to experience the Realm of God?' Jesus asked. And he gave us a way. Most of his teachings were pretty straightforward—easy to understand; not so easy to do, however. He said: *Repent*, take responsibility for what is wrong in your life and change the course; *trust* the universe, it will always provide; *forgive*, and be free from your demons; free yourself from the *judgment* of others; *love* compassionately and abundantly; have a *generous heart* with your time and money; do not be afraid to *take a costly stand for the justice* of the less privileged; and for God's sake never miss an opportunity to *celebrate and give thanks* for the gift of life."

And as Krister Stendahl, New Testament scholar, former dean of Harvard Divinity School, and bishop of the Church of Sweden, concluded: "So we must learn to sing our song to Jesus Christ with abandon, without telling negative stories about others. For it is simply not true that our faith and our devotion would be weakened by recognizing the insights and the beauty and the truths in other faiths. . . . I do not need to hate all other women to prove that I love my wife. Quite the contrary. The very attitude of contempt or condescension or negativism towards others pollutes the love of one's own.

"I sometimes wonder what will happen to all our adjectives when God mends and redeems and restores the Creation. For in the ultimate sense there can be no 'Christian' or 'Muslim' truth. Things are either true or not true. And to speak about the 'Christian God' is really careless shorthand for 'the conceptions and perceptions of God that scholars have found in Christianity.' But when we worship God, then there is only one God, however perceived through time and space. God beyond adjectives and partial claims, is not that what those famous words point to: 'God is spirit and those who worship him must worship him in spirit and in truth' (John 4:24)?"[56]

CHAPTER 9

THE USE AND ABUSE
OF THE BIBLE

"A religion without mystery must be a religion without God."
—JEREMY TAYLOR
ENGLISH BISHOP (1613)

A cartoon I vividly remember which appeared in *The New Yorker* portrays a man making inquiry at the counter of a large bookstore. The clerk, peering into her computer screen, says, "The Bible? Let's see, that would be in the 'Self Help' section."

A poll at the turn of the millennium reported that 10% of Americans believe that Joan of Arc was Noah's wife . . . 16% that the New Testament contains a book by the Apostle Thomas . . . only four in ten Americans know that Jesus delivered the Sermon on the Mount . . . and only three in ten teenagers know why Easter is celebrated.

Many modern Christians, claims Harvard University preacher Peter Gomes, are like the Emperor Charlemagne who, it is said, slept with a copy of Saint Augustine's magnum opus, *The City of*

God, under his pillow in the hope that this passive proximity to a great but difficult work might be of some benefit to him.[57]

Sadly, that is often the case. As Bill Coffin put it, "too many Christians use the Bible as a drunken individual does a lamp post—more for support than illumination!" How many times have you and I picked up a Bible and read little pieces of it, not in order to have it challenge our point of view—or God forbid, change our mind—but to have it confirm our prejudices and club our enemies?

I saw this happen just a few weeks after the devastation of September 11, 2001, when a zealous evangelist handed me a "Bible tract." It pictures the World Trade Center on fire with an American flag flying over it. Smoke pours out of the twin tours. Underneath is the caption, "America Under Attack . . . Who Can Protect Us?" It goes on to say, "The Bible predicts some horrific events which will foreshadow and culminate toward the end of civilization" (which the author clearly believes is at hand).

"The Bible," continues the tract, "also predicts Jesus's return to rescue those who profess their faith in Him. . . ." So in order to avoid eternal damnation, the reader is to pray, "Oh, God, at times like this, the world is such an awful place to live. . . . I just want to put my trust in You to get me through this life and to let me enter heaven once this life is over."

This is not the gospel of the love of God in Christ. This is an appeal to our most primitive fears, to get us to believe what is not true about the Bible or Christ or the world. The Bible was not written to get us out of the world to meet God "above" the world. It was written to encourage us to experience God "in" the world. And the forever-lasting life that Christ offers is here and now, not just there and then. "Christ in you, the hope of glory," as Paul puts it.[58] Further, God's salvation is not for Christians only, but for all people. As Paul wrote to young Timothy, "For to this end we toil and struggle, because we have our hope set on the living God, who is the Savior of *all people*, especially of those who believe."[59]

One of the most profound discoveries that the great physician, Dr. Karl Menninger, ever made was the truth that living with ambiguity is one of the determinants of adulthood. Unlike children, who require absolute answers to every question, or adolescents, who refuse to accept anyone else's answers, healthy adult behavior understands that truth is multi-faceted and that there is more than one way to understand reality.

Let me say unequivocally that the Bible has within it a good deal of ambiguity and contradiction. Case in point is the Biblical admonition of Psalm 46:10 "to be still and know that I am God." The context of this teaching was not the quiet contemplation of God in the serenity of a rose garden; it is set in the midst of an all out attack on you by your enemy. The idea is that God will protect you and fight for you.

Then contrast that with I Samuel 15: "Now therefore listen to the words of the Lord. Thus says the Lord of hosts, 'Now go and attack Amalek, and utterly destroy all that they have; do not spare them, but kill both man and woman, child and infant, ox and sheep, camel and donkey.'"

Take, as another example, one of the most quoted passages of Scripture in the United States since September 11:

> *"They shall beat their swords into plowshares,*
> *And their spears into pruning hooks;*
> *Nation shall not lift up sword against nation,*
> *Neither shall they learn war any more." (Isaiah 2:4)*

The same text is repeated almost word-for-word in Micah 4:3.

But, the exact opposite Word of the Lord is pronounced by the prophet Joel:

> *"Proclaim this among the nations:*
> *Prepare war.*
> *Stir up the warriors.*
> *Let all the soldiers draw near,*
> *Let them all come up.*
> *Beat your plowshares into swords,*

And your pruning hooks into spears;
Let the weakling say, 'I am a warrior.'" (Joel 3:9-10).

When it comes to the Bible, every one of us is a selective literal-
ist. We read the same sacred text, but we see only what we want to
see and hear only what we want to hear. Scripture is often ambiguous. So how do you decide which word is the "Word of the Lord"
to you? And when?

"Conflict regarding how to see and read the Bible is the single
greatest issue dividing Christians in North America today," says
Marcus Borg. "On the one side of the divide are the fundamentalists and many conservative-evangelical Christians. On the other
side are moderate-to-liberal Christians, mostly in mainline denom-
inations. . . . The first group, who sometimes call themselves
'Bible-believing Christians,' typically see the Bible as the inerrant
and infallible Word of God. As one bumper sticker puts it, 'God
said it . . . I believe it . . . that settles it.'

"The second group of Christians, although they know with certainty that they cannot be Biblical literalists like the first group, is
often uncertain about what it means to say that the Bible is 'the
Word of God.'"[60]

So it is that you have two kinds of Muslims. On the one side are
the peace-loving devotees of the religion of Islam. And on the
other side is the Taliban version of it, which believes that God is
only on their side, that America is the Great Satan, and that
America's sins are to blame for her destruction.

On the one side, you have the peace-loving religion of Jesus.
And on the other side are Jerry Falwell and Pat Robertson saying
that God Almighty removed his curtain of protection from
America on September 11 at the World Trade Center and the
Pentagon because America did not obey the Word of God. Citing
pagans, abortionists, feminists, homosexuals, the American Civil
Liberties Union, and the People for the American Way, Falwell
said, "I point the finger in their face and say, 'You helped this happen!'" And while he later apologized for his tone, calling his words

"insensitive," "uncalled for," and "unnecessary," he still does not believe they are wrong. He says, "I should have mentioned the national sins without mentioning the organizations and persons by name."

Fifty plus years ago someone finally asked United States Senator Joe McCarthy a question that needs to be asked today of these so-called Christian leaders and their millions of followers: "At long last, sir, have you no shame? Have you no decency?"

People who claim to follow the "Word of the Lord" are showing us right now the worst and the best of religion. "There are people in each religion who hold their beliefs in a tightfisted way as if it were the only one that could be true," says Diana Eck in her book, *A New Religious America.* "There are also people in each religious tradition who hold their beliefs in an open-handed way, an invitational way, making their faith part of a complex and multi-religious world."[61]

The basic clash in the world today is the clash between fanaticism and tolerance, the open and the closed fist. "Every one of these religious traditions is a battleground now with a fringe of fanaticism and xenophobia," offers theologian Harvey Cox. "Every religion has its social justice vision, its ecumenical wing, the wing in which religion inspires compassion and concern for the weak. And then there is the other wing, the poisonous and rancid side of religion, especially when it mixes with nationalism.

Terrorism is not just "those zealots over there. Extreme Christian fundamentalism breeds its own violent cells of terrorists here at home. According to the Abortion Rights League, there have been 2,500 reported attacks and 55,000 acts of illegal disruption against medical clinics since the late 1970s in the United States. For a free society, fundamentalism poses the most basic of paradoxes: It flourished by tolerance, but tolerance is what it cannot tolerate."[62]

As William Sloane Coffin often said, "Most, if not all of us, tend to hold certainty closer than truth. We want to learn only what we already know. We want to become only what we already are. . . .

"Believers often divide the world between the believers and the ungodly. Hating the ungodly, therefore, is not a moral lapse of intolerance, it is a religious obligation. Why all this intolerance? Because, while the unknown is the mind's greatest need, uncertainty is the heart's greatest fear. So fearful, in fact, is uncertainty, that many people engage in 'premature closure,' to use a psychological phrase, preferring certainty to truth, and the purity of dogma to the integrity of love . . . who think, 'Now abide faith, hope, love, these three, but find security in believing that the greatest of these is FAITH.'

"What a distortion of the gospel is to have limited sympathies and unlimited certainties, when the very reverse, to have limited certainties and unlimited sympathies, appears to be not only more tolerant but more Christian.

"The opposite of love is not hatred. The opposite of love is fear. But 'perfect love casts out fear.' [I John 4:18] Nothing scares me like scared people. For while love seeks the truth, fear seeks safety . . . which so often lies in the kind of divisive dogmatism and pitiless intolerance, which has characterized the Christian Church for years."[63]

To my reader, I would ask you to remember one thing: Thinking Christians believe in the Word made Flesh, not in the Word made Words. Everything in Christ is God-like, but everything in the Bible is not Christ-like. And always remember that no Word of God is God's last word.

When the prophet Jeremiah talks about "knowing God," he does not have in mind the sort of knowledge born of curiosity and control. He has in mind a type of knowledge which comes out of love. Faith is a relational word of trust more than a cerebral word of intellect. The more we open ourselves to experience the life and love of God through other people, the more we know God.

Somewhere along the way, in our quest to analyze, quantify, and figure out God, we stopped worshipping, stopped wondering, stopped reverencing, stopped encountering, and stopped serving our awesome God of the Bible as revealed to us through Jesus.

Faith is not believing without proof; it is trusting without reservation. Christianity is less a set of beliefs than it is a way of life. The Bible is our primary, though not exclusive, guide and illumination on this path.

Progressive Christians are not "Bibliolaters." We read the Bible, but we do not worship the Bible. We worship the God to whom the Bible points. The Bible is a signpost, not a hitching post. It points beyond itself, saying, "Pay attention to God, not to me." The Bible, as Richard Niebuhr taught, is "an indispensable means seeking its dispensability.

We progressives take the Bible much too seriously to take it literally. We know that our society is in search of spiritual and moral grounding in the midst of shifting values and moral chaos. So we are not going to trivialize the Bible, nor will we idolize it. Rather, we seek to enter into the Biblical story and allow it to enter into us, most particularly those of us who have been excluded from the faith of the Bible by the church's wrong use of the Bible.

The Bible seeks to open a discussion, but not to close it. It helps us ask the right questions, but does not give us all the answers. The Bible is not for those who think they already know what it means. The Bible is not for those who merely read it to garner support for their positions, but it is for those who are willing to risk the possibility that their positions may be wrong. The Bible is not simply a book to read; it is a book that reads us.

Martin Luther often called the Bible "the straw of the cradle in which the Christ child is laid." A cradle without its human contents is simply a piece of wood. "In Christ," said John Calvin, "are hidden 'all treasures of wisdom and knowledge' . . . not in the Bible save it leads us to Him."

Maybe it is as simple as a young man who is in love. He has a girlfriend who has captured his heart. As a result he carries a photograph of his beloved in his wallet because it reminds him of her when she is far away. Sometimes, when nobody is looking, he might even take out the photograph and give it a little kiss. But kissing a faded, wrinkled photograph is a poor substitute for the real thing.

And so it is with the Bible. Kissing the Bible is a poor substitute for the real thing. Better that we kiss the stars and the earth, the animals and their Creator. Better yet, that we kiss one another!

On the night before his fatal heart attack in 1965, Paul Tillich, the great American philosopher and theologian, was asked the same question that I have been discussing. "Dr. Tillich, the student asked, "do you believe the Bible is God's Holy Word?" Without a pause, the theologian responded, "YES, if it grasps you. NO, if you grasp it."

CHAPTER 10

PREPARATION
FOR DIVERSITY

One of Aesop's Fables tells of a snake that made its hole close to the porch of a cottage, whereupon the snake bit the cottager's son, causing his death. In his grief and anger, the cottager struck at the snake with his ax but only managed to cut off the snake's tail.

After some time, the cottager, afraid lest the snake should bite him, tried to make peace with the snake. To which the snake replied, "There can henceforth be no peace between us; for whenever I see you I shall remember the loss of my tail, and whenever you see me you will be thinking of the death of your son."

How we choose to see things makes a world of difference, literally.

Another view of snakes and humans was envisioned by Edward Hicks, the American Quaker preacher and folk artist. He painted his well-known theme, "The Peaceable Kingdom," in about 60 different versions. His personal favorite, and most popular rendition, was painted in 1844.

You know the themes of the painting: God's peaceable kingdom on earth when the lion will lie down with the lamb and all the wild and domestic creatures will be led in peace by a child. Nearly all the "Peaceable Kingdom" paintings contain a version of William Penn's treaty with the Indians. Hicks believed that in Penn's "holy experiment" in Pennsylvania lay the seeds for fulfilling the Biblical prophecy of heaven on earth.

The scripture which inspired him to this religious optimism was the text from Isaiah 11. Israel's vision of peace was a state of earthly bounty and well-being that stemmed from living under God's rule. It was a vision of concord and harmony, order, security, and prosperity. For Isaiah and the other prophets, the messianic king sent by God would be "prince of peace" (Isaiah 9:6), who would "command peace to the nations" (Zechariah 9:10). The very word, "Jerusalem," connotes "city of peace."

Tragically, to this day, not even Jerusalem recognizes what Jesus called "the things that make for peace" (Luke 19:42).

How we see things makes all the difference.

Perhaps the Swiss psychoanalyst, Alice Miller, can help us see things differently. In her book, *For Your Own Good: Hidden Cruelty and the Roots of Violence*, she sees a direct relationship between child-rearing practices and adult violence. She calls it "poisonous pedagogy."

The key to adult violence, she suggests, does not lie in the experience of a particular childhood trauma, but rather in whether or not the child, either through fear of withdrawal of love or through overt force, was compelled to suppress the feeling aroused by such trauma. "Those who were permitted to react appropriately throughout their childhood—i.e. with anger—to the pain, wrongs and denial inflicted upon them . . . will retain this ability to react appropriately in later life too. When someone wounds them as adults, they will be able to recognize and express this verbally. But they will not feel the need to lash out in response. This need arises only for people who must always be on their guard to keep the dam that restrains their feelings from breaking. . . . A person who can understand and integrate his anger as part of himself will not become violent."

Miller says that "all advice that pertains to raising children betrays more or less clearly the numerous, variously clothed needs of the adult [for power, control, and continuance of the inherited behavior]. Fulfillment of these needs not only discourages the child's development but actually prevents it. This holds true when the adult is honestly convinced of acting in the child's best interests. . . ." [as in corporal punishment. When children are hit, they learn to hit others.]

"When children are trained, they learn to train others in turn. Children who are lectured to, learn how to lecture; if they are admonished, they learn how to admonish; if scolded, they learn how to scold; if ridiculed, they learn how to ridicule; if humiliated, they learn how to humiliate; if their psyche is killed, they will learn how to kill—the only question is who will be killed: oneself, others, or both."[64]

If she is right, the greatest preparation we can make for the coming of Christ and his Peaceable Kingdom might well be to begin to get in touch as individuals, families, and nations with the bottled-up hurt and anger of our pasts. We do not have to carry on the sins of our fathers and mothers, or of their religion. We can break the cycle of thousands of years of violence in our lifetime. Think how differently *Romeo and Juliet* would have turned out if their families had broken the vicious cycle of violence. What about Protestants and Catholics in Northern Ireland? Israelis and Palestinians in the Middle East? Whites and non-whites? Heterosexuals and homosexuals? "Developed" and "underdeveloped" countries?

Is it humanly possible that lambs can lie down with wolves and wake up alive? Is it humanly possible for a nursing child to play with a poisonous snake and not die? Is it humanly possible for a youth to have more wisdom than all the generals at the Pentagon?

No! It is not humanly possible. But with God, all things are possible.

Martin Luther King, Jr. began one of his most famous sermons with the assertion that, "At the center of the Christian faith is the conviction that in the universe there is a God of power who is able to do exceedingly abundant things in nature and in history."[65] *He* believed that.

It will make all the difference in the world if *we* believe that.

"There can henceforth be no peace between us [replied Aesop's snake to the cottager]; for whenever I see you I shall remember the loss of my tail, and whenever you see me you will be thinking of the death of your son."

We can choose to believe that perception, generation after generation, and let it be our sorry legacy to our children's children.

Or we can choose to believe the Psalmist: "Thou [the Lord] preparest a table before me in the presence of mine enemies. . . . My cup runneth over.

Likewise the Lord's Supper [communion] is the most radical social act we will ever take part in. At the communion table we give up past hurts and wrongs and open ourselves up to a new way of living. This table of grace is available to us because one Human Being ran the risk of love in the face of the world's hate. His life and love flow down from the cross and into us. When we partake of this feast, we sit at a table in the presence of the Risen Christ with people around the world and next door to us, whom we would never, ever invite to our own homes for dinner.

When we leave this communion table, we are prepared to go back to our kitchen tables and our conference tables in the strength of the one who said, "You have hurt me and I have bled, but I stand here eye to eye and declare to you that I forgive you. Let us put the past behind us and join hands for the future."

The Gospel risk is to face an old enemy, and to drop our guard, and see if the snake will still strike. What a loss it will be for our generation if we do not take the risk.

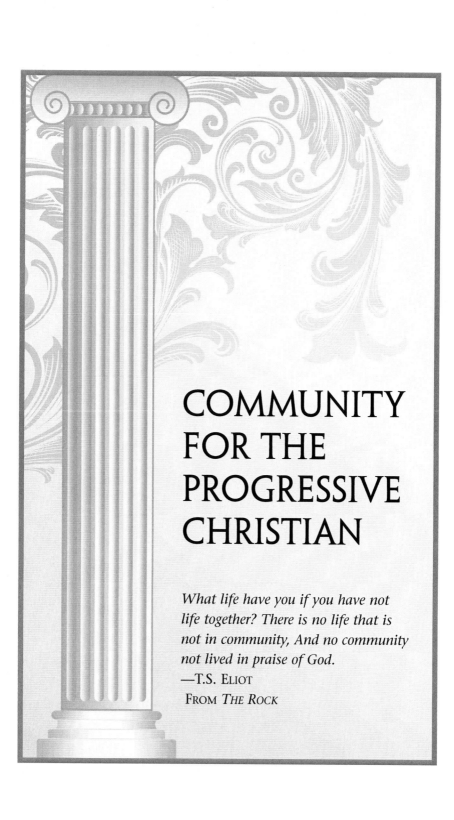

COMMUNITY
FOR THE
PROGRESSIVE
CHRISTIAN

*What life have you if you have not
life together? There is no life that is
not in community, And no community
not lived in praise of God.*
—T.S. ELIOT
FROM *THE ROCK*

CHAPTER 11

KNOW THAT OUR BEHAVIOR REFLECTS OUR BELIEF

Remember Eliza Doolittle in *My Fair Lady* when she lashes out at Freddy as well as Henry Higgins? "Words, words, words! I'm so sick of words. I get words all day through, first from him, now from you. Don't talk of stars burning above. Don't talk of love. Show me. SHOW ME NOW!"

Eliza sang those words because she knew that when all is said and done, more is said than done. And that is why the Eight Points of Progressive Christianity are committed to action, not just to talk. "By calling ourselves progressive, we mean that we are Christians who know that the way we behave toward one another and toward other people is the fullest expression of what we believe."

Christianity is not about believing the correct doctrines; it is about living like our Leader. The Jesus we meet in the gospels is a man of action, who heals, who demonstrates compassion, who takes a stand against injustices, who loves unconditionally, and who then tells his disciples to go and do likewise. Maybe that is why the writers of all three synoptic gospels wrote that Jesus believed that the most important commandment in the Bible is to "love God with all of our hearts and to love our neighbor as we love ourselves."[66]

So, how do we go about "loving our neighbor as we love ourselves"? That brings us to the next point:

"We are Christians who form ourselves into communities educated to equipping one another for the work we are called to do: striving for peace and justice among all people, protecting and restoring the integrity of God's creation, and bringing hope to those Jesus called the least of his sisters and brothers."

In Genesis 12, God tells Abraham that he and his family will be "blessed to be a blessing" to the nations. "In you all the families of the earth (literally) shall bless themselves."

I venture to guess that many people are committed to putting "family first." The question raised by our understanding of Progressive Christianity, however, is: "How large is your family? Who are you first and foremost?

> . . . a member of your birth family?
> . . . a member of your town?
> . . . a member of your business?
> . . . a member of America?
> . . . or are you first and foremost a member of humanity?"

Jesus constantly challenged his followers to widen their circle of concern to take in all human beings. There is often a tension, however, between the responsibility we owe to our own families, and that which we owe to our wider families, those whom Jesus called "the least of these."

According to the Gospel of Mark, the account of Jesus's life written closest to it (from stories of people whose grandparents might have actually met him), Jesus had nothing particularly positive to say about natural families and everything positive to say about the larger human family. When Jesus was informed that his mother and brothers were waiting outside the lecture hall, asking for him, he replied, "Who are my mother and my brothers [and my sisters]?"

He repudiated his own nuclear family in favor of his new world family, his wider family of all of those most in need—the child, the widowed, the lonely, the sick, the hungry, the foreigner, the immigrant, the oppressed, the prisoner—even the enemy.

People have a natural instinct to look after their blood relatives. And this is good. This "kin altruism," as it is called, appears to be genetically driven. You see it throughout most of the species.

What is not good is when we only look after our own. "Katie, Bar the Door! Us Four, No More!" But Jesus challenges his followers to widen their circle of concern to take in all human beings.

The "Us Four, No More" ethic is built entirely on the fear of scarcity. That fear restricts us to only providing for our loved ones. But Jesus replaces that ethic with the "Whatsoever You Do Unto the Least of These, You Do Unto Me" ethic of plenty. The first makes us uptight, fearful, stingy, and greedy. The second makes us open, free, generous, and benevolent.

"Jesus experienced God in a profoundly intimate way as the 'Parent of All Creation.' He had a clear vision about the interconnectedness of all life. He recognized every human being as a child of God. Any other identifying factor was secondary to that truth and likely a distraction (i.e., family, wealth, status, position). As a child of God, every human deserves dignity and justice regardless of his or her status in this world. Anything less would be an affront to God or a sin against God."[67]

How we experience God will determine what we do about God's world. The eighth and final point in our Progressive Christianity states that, "We are Christians who recognize that being followers of Jesus is costly, and entails selfless love, conscientious resistance to evil, and renunciation of privilege—as has always been the tradition of the church."

Having been in this business of ministry most of my adult life, I have come to the conclusion that there are a number of Christians whose idea of spirituality is just weird! They walk around with their heads in the skies. I sometimes think they are so "heavenly-minded" that they are of no earthly good!

My primary faculty advisor for my Doctoral Thesis at Princeton had a name for the opposite of this heavenly-minded "other-worldliness." He called it the "This-Worldliness" of the Gospel. And I understand what he meant. Jesus taught us to pray, not about going to heaven, but about heaven coming through us. "Thy kingdom come [here], Thy will be done [here], on earth as it is in heaven!"

Compassion often demands confrontation. Although most churches vastly prefer charity, which in no way affects the status quo, to justice, which often leads to political and economic confrontation.

We cannot say that we love the Jesus . . .

. . . Who tore down the walls of oppression in his day,

. . . Who spoke out and acted out against the civil and religious authorities,

. . . Who refused to pay back the religious violence of an eye for an eye and a tooth for a tooth,

. . . And who told us that our well-being is inextricably tied to the well-being of those less fortunate . . .

Unless we seek to demonstrate to some degree Jesus's godly compassion and confrontation in our own lives as well as in the world.

What happens in church on a Sunday morning is a "Pep Rally" for what needs to happen in the world throughout the week.

Abraham Joshua Heschel, arguably the greatest Jewish leader in our time, made the following critique of religion:

"Religion declined not because it was refuted,
but because it became irrelevant,
dull, oppressive, insipid.

When faith is completely replaced by creed,
worship by discipline, love by habit;
When the crisis of today is ignored;
because of the splendor of the past;
When faith becomes an heirloom,
other than a living fountain;
When religion speaks only in the name of authority
rather than with the voice of compassion,
its message becomes meaningless."

Martin Luther King, Jr. had it right: "If the Church of today does not recapture the sacrificial spirit of the early Church, it will lose its authentic ring, forfeit the loyalty of millions, and be dismissed as an irrelevant social club with no meaning for the [21st] Century."

Each of us needs a tough mind and a tender heart. And that may well mean agreeing to disagree. But through study groups and sharing our stories with one another, we can translate personal faith into public challenge and give voice to the voiceless and dis-enfranchised.

"When all hearts are one, nothing else need be."[68]

Through hands-on partnership projects within the ministries within a specific church and of the church with local, national, and world organizations, we can share our lives with others in common-cause and long-term relationships. We need to care for God's creation and humanity. The possibilities are unlimited.

"If you forget everything else that has been said," said Thomas Merton, "I would suggest you remember this for the future:

'From now on, everybody stands on his/her own feet.'"

You and I can help make that happen . . . and we will!

CHAPTER 12

TAKING
CALCULATED RISKS

Sister Monica inherited $100 from an elderly aunt. She asked permission of the Mother Superior to give the money to a needy person. The Mother Superior said she thought that just fine. So Sister Monica went out in front of the convent and spotted a downtrodden-looking man, identified herself as Sister Monica from the convent, and said, "I want you to take this," and handed him a $100 bill. She patted him on the shoulder and said, "Godspeed."

The man was shocked, but put the money in his pocket and went on. Late that afternoon he reappeared at the convent door and asked for Sister Monica. She came out and he handed her $1,000. She was amazed, and said, "What's this? I don't understand!"

Looking at her admiringly, he said, "Godspeed paid off ten to one!"[69]

Sister Monica took a high risk. She gave away everything she had. And the R.O.I., her Return on Investment, came back tenfold.

This could be a current day interpretation of Jesus's Parable of the Coins, or the Talents. Matthew, a former tax collector, tells Jesus's story just before the beginning of the Passion narrative. In Luke, a version of this story occurs right after Jesus's encounter with Zacchaeus, the wealthy businessman, and right after Palm Sunday.

Let's have more fun retelling the parable. There is a corporate executive who is taking off to Japan. She calls together her three investment managers and "divides her substance among them." In a single act of wild, extravagant, risky grace, she takes off without a penny in her pocket, only a round-trip plane ticket. Just when they need her most for advice to tell them how best to invest the money entrusted to them, she's gone.

Managers 1 and 2 go to work investing their shares on some pretty high-risk venture capital opportunities. The third one is cautious. He plays it safe. Too much at stake to risk it, he thinks.

Now, before we become too critical of this guy, let's try to put ourselves in his place. He was given a full talent. That is a sum of money equivalent to 15 years of labor. That's a lot of money. Figure it up. At minimum wage, it's over $100,000. I read not too long ago that the average annual family income in New Canaan is close to $175,000. (I know what you're thinking right now, "That sure isn't my income!") So, let's give ourselves the benefit of the doubt and drop it down $100,000—with two wage earners in the family, that's $50,000 each. Conservatively, that's like being given $750,000—3/4 of a million dollars. Or take your earnings for a year and put a zero on the right-hand side. That's ten times. Make it 50% greater than that. That's how much this guy was given.

Now, what are you going to do with that much money, especially if it was in tens? You couldn't wire it to your bank. It wasn't a cashier's check. It was hard, cold cash. Picture it. Don't worry about investing it—how are you even going to get it home? Put it under your coat? That's an easy mark! Let's say you drag it along in one of those big green garbage bags.

Then when you get it home, what do you do with it? Put it under the bed? You would be up and down all night, checking the door lock, listening for noises. So, let's say you decide to bury it in the backyard, under your children's sandbox.

Finally, your boss returns. Your colleague #1 says to her, "You gave me the equivalent of 75 years of wages. I doubled it for you— here it is."

"Well done," she says. "You were faithful over a little; I will give you more responsibility. Enter into the joy of your position as C.O.O."

Colleague #2 says, "You gave me 30 years of wages. I doubled it for you—here it is."

"Well done," she says. You were faithful over a little; I will give you more responsibility. Enter into the joy of your new corner office."

Now she smiles expectantly at you. You say, "Wait, I'll be right back." An hour later, you struggle into her office, perspiring profusely, dragging behind you that green bag with dirt all over it. "Here you go," you say. "I kept all the money. I didn't waste any of it. I didn't spend anything on myself. I didn't play the lottery or give it to my cronies. I didn't give one cent to anybody. I knew you were tough, so I was afraid to waste it. So here is every cent you gave me—intact!"

And the boss replies, "You wicked and lazy manager! You knew I wanted to see some return on my investment. The least you could have done was to have invested my money in the bank at 5-1/2%. So take this money, clean the dirt off of it, and give it to my two other managers here."

Then comes that terrible phrase, "To those who have shall more be given. And from those who have not, even the little they have shall be taken away."

What do you think about a statement like that? In our world where less than 10% of the people already get more than 90% of the earth's resources—where the rich continue to get richer while the poor get poorer—what do you do with a statement like that? Better yet, what do you do with a God whose son talks like that?

The fact is that it was never that man's money, or talent, or skill to begin with. They were all wonderful gifts of grace from God. His only job was to invest it all for the good of others. And the terrible lesson is that we, like he, could lose it faster than we made it.

When we lose our *sense* of whose we are and whose gifts we have been given, it isn't long before we lose our *soul*.

In one of my former churches, we were serving bag lunches to upwards of 75 people a day who had ended up for one reason or another on the streets. One third of them were children. Our staff social worker and I wanted to bring the folks, many of whom we knew by name, into the church dining room, serve them a hot meal in a warm, safe place—maybe even provide a little piano music so that they might keep what little was left of their dignity and self-respect. We took it to the trustees, but they said no. It would be too expensive, they said, to secure the doors into the rest of the church and to clean up after them.

We proposed that we allow some of the homeless folks to use the bathrooms and showers in our gym, especially those who were trying to look presentable for job interviews. But the trustees said no. It would cost too much money, and we would lose the income from the groups of white-collar workers who played basketball there after work.

We proposed that we turn an unused basement into a center for children's day care, mental health counseling, and job placement. We couldn't do it. It would cost too much.

We had to fire a part-time youth director because they didn't want all those latchkey kids running wild in the church. Same story. Couldn't do it. "We have a sacred trust here," they said. A former Chairman of the Board once said to me, "I love this church—every stone and stained glass in it. It's the people I can't tolerate."

Hell is truth seen too late. Whether it is buildings or budgets, possessions or professional careers, "To whom much is given, much is required."

Every *thing* we have is a gift from God.
Every *dime we ever earned* is a gift from God.
Every *talent* we have is a gift from God.
Every *personal attribute* we possess is a gift from God.
Every bit of *knowledge and education* we have gained is a gift
    from God.
Every *sphere of influence* we can touch is a gift from God.

All of it is a pure gift from God. And it was all given us to be
shared with others. What we do with what we have determines
whether we can be trusted to manage more of it.

In fact, it is really the boss who is most at risk in Jesus's story.
She has entrusted her whole life, everything she has and has to
offer, to her managers. If she is to accomplish anything for anybody, it is up to them. Here is a story of extravagant grace and vulnerability told by the most extravagant one of all as he begins his
long journey toward a place called Calvary.

We serve a God who loves to trust us, even when we blow it
. . . a God who cares for us, even when we are too *careless* and
when we are too *careful*.

"The third servant got the risk, but he never got the gift. If you
sense only the risk, but don't receive the gift, the grace, there is
nowhere to go except to the back yard in fear, in trembling fear.
Once the money got buried, there was no decision to be made. It
was over. No defeat, no possibility of victory of elation, no exhilarating risk, no joy, no sorrow, no grace. There's nothing but a [big]
hole and a whole lot of money."[70]

Maureen Dowd wrote a great column in the *New York Times*. She
called it "Ted's Excellent Idea." She interviewed Ted Turner, who
gave away over $200 million to charity in 1994. "My hand shook
when I signed the papers," he says, "because I knew I was taking
myself out of the running for the richest man in America."

Instead of the joy of giving, he was consumed by the fear of
falling—falling off "The Forbes Four Hundred List" of wealthiest
Americans. But he learned that giving can be as much fun as mak-

ing, and now he wants his fellow billionaires—or 'ol' skinflints,' as he calls them—to 'open their purse strings' wider.

"That list is destroying our country!" he bellows cheerfully over the phone. "These new super-rich won't loosen up their wads because they're afraid they'll reduce their net worth and go down on the list. That's their Super Bowl."

Turner asks a profound question: "Why isn't it better to be the biggest giver rather than the biggest hog?" So he suggests we start an annual list of the most generous givers in the U.S., and offer an "Ebenezer Scrooge Prize" that embarrasses stingy billionaires and a "Heart of Gold Award" that honors philanthropists.

He talked to Bill Gates, the Microsoft founder, and Warren Buffett, the two richest men in the country, and he claims that they would be inclined to give more if there was a list of who did the giving rather than the having. Mr. Gates promises to give away most of his $16 billion, but he wants to wait until he is 50 or 60 to plan it. Mr. Buffett says he will give the bulk of his $15 billion to population control, but not until he and his wife are dead. Mr. Turner insists that "tomorrow is not another day, when it comes to population and the environment. THEY SHOULD DO IT NO-O-OW!"[71] Apparently, Mr. Turner wielded a lot of influence because the media are now full of ways Bill and Melinda Gates and Warren Buffett are generously using their money to provide for philanthropic causes.

I think that's a great idea! Not just for the mega-rich, but for all of us. Think of the millions of people who could be given a "leg up," not just a "hand out,"—a new start, not just a Happy Meal. Think of the tremendous Return on Investment for the people of the world that would occur if we in this country made giving more fashionable than hoarding.

If I read Jesus correctly, those who guard their assets and bury their treasures and talents get exactly what they've earned: ZIP! But those who invest their assets in others and distribute their wealth of time, treasure, and talents for the good of all get what they have earned: the great joy of doing even more of it.

The Kingdom of Heaven doesn't consist of buying and selling, but of giving and receiving.

Hooray for the Ted Turners out there. You and I may never be in the Top 10 on his new list. In fact, no one may ever know all the many ways in which we have invested our lives—but *we know*!

And I have a hunch that Sister Monica was right. "Godspeed" pays off.

Ten to one!

CHAPTER 13

NO MORE "SOUR GRAPES"

"Things have a way of falling to pieces. The shingles blow off the roof. The fender rusts through and the exhaust pipe drags. Cuffs fray, nylons run, hair falls out, joints stiffen, and wattles appear under our chins. Nothing is exempt, not even our ideas.

"Athens begins with a great and democratic vision, and finishes in ruin and ignominy. Arthur begins with a high vision of a knightly fellowship, and it all ends in perfidy. Washington and Jefferson have an exhilarating idea for a new kind of nation, and it progresses to the tumidity and bathos of the Great Society."[72]

The fairest legal system on earth has become hostage to the entertainment media. Justice is eclipsed by economic gain and racist political maneuvering. Passion is rampant toward what cannot be done while compassion is reduced to private charity.

Over fifty years ago in 1945, men and women of humanitarian and moral stature founded the first international organization for peace and justice. Today the United Nations stands at a crossroads, reeling from decades of internal conflicts and disorganization and from the external warring of nation-states over land and power. The world's greatest hope for sanity and order has been reduced to nationalistic myopia, petty bickering, and personal temper tantrums.

Yet, in spite of the evidence, we have hope. As the abolitionist preacher Theodore Parker, put it, "The arc of the moral universe is long, but it bends toward justice." And it is justice, not charity, that is wanting in the world.

"I will seek the lost, and I will bring back the strayed, and I will bind up the injured and I will strengthen the weak, but the fat and the strong I will destroy," says the Lord, "I will feed them with justice." (Ezekiel 34:16)

As Abraham Lincoln asked in his First Inaugural Address, "Why should there not be a patient confidence in the ultimate justice of the people? Is there any better or equal hope in the world?"

So, even though things have a way of falling to pieces, God has a way of getting us to glue it all back together again. Jesus's persistent widow who cries day and night to a crooked judge finally gets justice, and that quickly.

> *"But mercy is above this sceptered sway,*
> *It is enthroned in the hearts of kings,*
> *It is an attribute to God Himself,*
> *And earthly power doth then show likest God's*
> *When mercy seasons justice," said Shakespeare.*[73]

So, if down deep we know that justice is the best medicine, why don't we practice it?

I found some help in this recently in reading a lecture given several years ago by Arthur Leff, a brilliant Yale law professor who has since died of cancer. His lecture was titled, "Unspeakable Ethics, Unnatural Law." He told his fellow lawyers,

"I want to believe—and so do you—in a complete, transcendent and immanent set of propositions about right and wrong, *findable* rules that authoritatively and unambiguously direct us how to live righteously. I also want to believe—and so do you—in no such thing, but rather that we are wholly free, not only to choose for ourselves what we ought to do, but to decide for ourselves, individually and as a species, what we ought to be. What we want, Heaven help us, is simultaneously to be perfectly ruled and perfectly free, that is, at the same time to discover the right and the good and to create it."[74]

In other words, we want it both ways. We want to have our cake of universally valid moral rules and eat it too by being free to do whatever we choose. Leff pointed out the assumption in each scenario of an "unevaluated evaluator": either God or our own human reason. His dilemma was that he could not accept either as his source of ultimate law. He concluded his lecture by saying:

"All I can say is this: it looks as if we are all we have. Given what we know about ourselves, and each other, this is an extraordinarily unappetizing prospect: looking around the world, it appears that if all men are brothers, the ruling model is Cain and Abel. Neither reason, nor love, nor even error, seems to have worked to make us 'good,' and worse than that, there is no reason why anything should. Only if ethics were something unspeakable by us could law be unnatural, and therefore unchangeable. As things stand now, everything is up for grabs.

"Nevertheless:
- *Napalming babies is bad.*
- *Starving the poor is wicked.*
- *Buying and selling each other is depraved.*
- *Those who stood up and died resisting Hitler, Stalin, Amin, and Pol Pot—and General Custer too—have earned salvation.*
- *Those who acquiesced deserve to be damned.*
- *There is in the world such thing as evil."[75]*

Says who? You see the problem? God help us.

In Jeremiah 31 God promises to rewrite the rules. There was a popular proverb in those days that went, "The fathers have eaten sour grapes and the children's teeth are set on edge" (or more probably 'blunted'). In other words, "What's the use of trying—our ancestors have done wrong and we are paying the price!" We hear the same kind of excuses today:

It's not my fault!
Look what you made me do!
She was abused as a child.
He was driven mad by racial hatred.
Look what she was wearing! She was asking for it.
If you didn't defy me, I wouldn't have to beat you.
He was on sugar overload, so he killed.
It was because he had a drinking problem.
He was depressed/obsessed/oppressed, so he stole/stalked/
    stomped.

It is as though we have never heard of free will! As a society we have just about given up taking responsibility for our actions. Our teeth are blunted because of something our parents did. Now, clearly, there are things that happen to us which are beyond our control. But the vast majority of us are responsible for our own actions. We are not predestined by circumstances. Folks, we have got to stop playing the victim and passing the buck of personal responsibility. When we make mistakes and do wrong, we need to be human enough to admit it, repent, and make it right. We are accountable for what we do with what God has given us. Accountability is the essence of being human and being free.

When Jeremiah wrote this, Israel had been devastated, plucked up, sent off into exile. Its cities were unlivable (much like today). The prophet foresaw a day when its cities would be rebuilt and life restored. He called it the "New Covenant."

Remember that the old covenant, the law given to Moses, was a way that Israel should live so that she could be a light to all the other nations who did not know God. Time and again it was broken, not just the stone tablets, but the spirit of the law. So God promises a "new covenant," a law within them, written on their hearts. It was not a different law; the law was to become an integral part of them. No longer would they have to check a law book to see if stealing or pagan worship was wrong. They would know it in their hearts.

"The only means you and I have of rising above the tooth, claw, and nail existence to which we moderns have sunk is the Torah, the law of God." As Christians and Jews, we are "to live lives that witness to a loving God, an 'unevaluated evaluator,' who stands above us and beyond us so that [that God] might stand truly for us and with us."[76]

That strength to know what is right and do it, to stand against evil in all of its modern forms, to love in the face of hate, is the "New Covenant" in your hearts. We know it is so because we have seen it embodied in the person of Jesus Christ and in the heart of the sacrament of his self-giving love.

C. S. Lewis said that "Duty is only a substitute for love (of God and other people), like a crutch, which is a substitute for a leg. Most of us need the crutch at times; but of course it's idiotic to use the crutch when our own legs (our own loves, tastes, habits, etc.) can do the journey on their own!"[77]

"If you forget everything else that has been said," said Thomas Merton, the great spiritual guide of our generation, "I would suggest you remember this for the future: 'From now on, everybody stands on his own feet.'"

We have a new covenant with God through Christ. We know what we need to do, whether in the U.N. or in our personal lives. Let us talk no more of "sour grapes." Nobody is helped by it. And it's not that great for our teeth either!

CHAPTER 14

IS PATIENCE A VIRTUE?

The light turns green at the busy intersection. The man's car stalls and he can't get the engine to turn over. A chorus of honking cars behind him makes matters worse. Finally, he gets out of his car, walks back to the first driver, and says, "I'm sorry, but I can't seem to get my car started. If you'll go up there and give it a try, I'll stay here and blow your horn for you!"

I know how both of those drivers felt.

They say patience is a virtue. That may well be true. But I have to tell you, if it is true, I not only have little patience, I have little virtue.

I hate to wait. I hate to wait in traffic, in lines, in crowds, on the phone, and at the D.M.V. They say all good things come to those who wait. I don't think so.

Too often I find myself praying the prayer of the modern American: "Dear God, I pray for patience. And I want it right now!"

It is the same with "peace on earth, goodwill toward men." Each year in the four weeks before Christmas sermons are preached about waiting for Jesus's birth. But "Advent" means "coming." It does not mean "waiting." If Advent means each of us waiting for somebody else to do it for us, it will never happen. It is not good enough to send beautiful little cards to each other wishing for it to happen.

And it is not good enough for the faithful just to show up at the right time, as though we were "Waiting for Godot" on the street corner. Because Godot hasn't decided to show up yet. And the time may come when we wonder it there really is a Godot or not.

Advent is a difficult concept for those of us who are activists. We want to make things happen now. When I am in a meeting and someone says, "We can't go any further with this until we talk to so-and-so," my first impulse is to walk over to the desk, pick up the phone, and call them right then. They might not be there, but I figure at least I have taken responsibility for that over which I have control.

Let us not fool ourselves. At the end of the day, what counts is what has been accomplished, not what has been wished for. Advent is helpful to the degree that our longing spurs us on to higher expectation; and our higher expectation to greater involvement.

One of the tragedies of Christian preaching at this time of year is the announcement that Jesus has fulfilled all the Jewish expectations for "the" Messiah, so there is nothing else to be done except to wait for his Second Coming. If He's already done it all, what is there left to do?

But the coming of the babe in Bethlehem is only the first phase of God's revelation through Christ. Christianity, like Judaism, is still waiting for God to complete the redemption of the world. What Christians call "the Second Coming" is strikingly similar to what the Bible and Jewish theology calls the great eschatological "Day of the Lord." And that day has not yet come.

While we believe that Jesus of Nazareth was the unique 'image and likeness' of God and is the savior of the world, we must agree with our Jewish brothers and sisters that the world is not yet redeemed. And it is not enough to keep saying to ourselves over and over again that it is. Jesus is a means by which God's love and call for justice are made known among the gentiles, even as God's love and will for justice have been known in Israel. Whether Christian or Jew or Muslim or whomever, we have the choice whether to become part of the process God is using to redeem the earth.

The world will not be saved by everyone celebrating Christmas. God comes into the world through the faith and action of human beings who make the attempt to do God's work and God's will. It is pretty safe to say that if we do not "prepare the way," and "make straight a highway for our God," God will not do it for us.

Patience is not one of the major Christian virtues. In the face of the world's hatred, greed, sexism, racism, illiteracy, poverty, war, the bloated bellies of starving children, patience is a terrible sin. Some of the world's greatest injustices are caused through too much patience. Every forty seconds an American woman is the victim of domestic violence. She has lived with the abuser for twenty years, twenty years of fear and hoping he might change. And we say to her, "Well, sometimes you just have to be patient!"

Every twenty-two minutes, some man, woman, or child around the world accidentally steps on an old $2.00 land mine, left in the ground after some skirmish, and has a leg blown off or is killed. "Collateral Damage," we call it. And we say to that dead child, or one-legged adult, "Well, those land mines will probably de-activate themselves in 75 years or so. Sometimes you just have to be patient."

What if Rosa Parks had been patient and just sat where she was supposed to sit? What if Gandhi had just been patient? Or George Washington? Or Martin Luther King, Jr.?

"We want peaceful homes, but what efforts do we put into mak-ing that happen? We complain about the violence on television and in the movies, yet we continue to expose ourselves to it. We worry about the violence in our children's lives, yet we buy toys that foster it. We disapprove of the greed and fierce competition in professional sports, but we still support them. . . . Our actions are sometimes inconsistent with our desires. We want peace yet we rarely step into the way of peace."[78]

Martin Luther King, Jr. never wrote a book on racial injustice entitled, *Why We Ought to Be Patient and Wait Another Two Hundred Years*.

Yet some things take time. Fundamental change requires time. The wheels of the gods grind slowly, but they grind exceedingly small. Fundamental change will not happen overnight.

In an interview several years ago, during the Korean nuclear crisis, former United Nations Ambassador Andrew Young was asked to comment on former President Carter's trip to talk with the North Koreans. He said, "This is the sort of situation which you can afford to talk to death. We ought to be willing to take all the time in the world with this one. We must be patient."[79]

Good parents know that. Child rearing takes patience. Rome wasn't built in a day. Neither were healthy, moral, loving young people. In his *Letter to the Romans*, Paul asks, "Where would we be if God were not patient, if God were unwilling to let us fail, stumble, and eventually grow toward God?" That God, he says, has infinite patience when it comes to us.

So, maybe we should be patient about some things. The Biblical prophets spoke out because they had their eyes fixed, not on the immediate situation, but on the future. They kept talking about the coming reign of God, all present evidence to the contrary, because they had patience . . . a patience born of their conviction that God lived, that God acted, that God cared, and that God would move toward God's people.

Emily Dickinson seemed to have that form of patience when she wrote:

"Hope is the thing with feathers
That perches in the soul,
And sings the tune without the words,
And never stops at all.

And sweetest in the gale is heard—
And sore must be the storm
that could abash the little bird
That kept so many warm.

I've heard it in the chilliest land,
And on the strangest sea;
Yet, never, in extremity,
It asked a crumb of me."

Several years ago, two young condors on the West Coast were hatched in captivity and grew in carefully constructed cages so as to allow their vast 10-foot wing span to develop. Once nearly extinct, there are now only 58 of these great vultures in existence.

The day they were released there were dozens of TV cameras focused on the workmen as they carefully dismantled the huge cage. Piece by piece it was carted away. The two condors stood proud in their places, black plumage and ruff of white feathers shimmering in the wind, their bare heads and necks turning suspiciously, nervously watching the removal of their "home."

Everyone anticipated that they would immediately leap into the air, spread their broad winds, pick up a warm, fast-moving current of wind and fly off into the endless blue sky. But it didn't happen! The two condors refused to budge. They just stood there. The trainers cajoled, shouted, jumped up and down, but the great birds would not move, would not lift a wing, would not fly—would not claim their freedom.

It took them 24 hours to run, leap, and fly. By that time all the cameras were gone. How sad. How blind! The world missed the real story.

As my friend, Rabbi Harvey Fields, tells it, the two condors had piously entered into prayer! They knew by instinct what each of us must learn. Liberation is a process, not an instant advent. Its sap rises slowly, painfully in us. Soaring high and free comes with patience, discipline, with the confidence to take risks, and with the wisdom to live with the consequences of our actions.[80]

"Hope is the thing with feathers
That perches in the soul,
And sings the tune without the words,
And never stops at all."

CHAPTER 15

A CLASH OF EMPIRES

"Lead us, Heavenly Father, lead us
O'er the world's tempestuous sea."
—JOHN EDMESTON
ENGLISH HYMN WRITER, 1852

In a recent column in the *New York Times*, Garry Wills asserts that
there is no such thing as "Christian politics." "If it is politics," he
claims, "it cannot be Christian. Jesus told Pilate: 'My reign is not
of this present order.' What would Jesus do?" Wills asks, and then
answers, "Stay away from politics!"[81]

I couldn't disagree more. Politics are literally, "the life of 'the
polis'—'the city.' If politics are not doing what they are supposed
to be doing, they should be changed, not discarded. Sometimes
the most effective political statement is one of symbolic religious
confrontation.

Such was the case on that spring day in the year 30 when two
entirely different processions entered the city of Jerusalem. It was
the beginning of the week of Passover, the most sacred week of the
Jewish year. One was a *peasant procession*, the other an *imperial procession*.[82]

Approaching Jerusalem from the East, Jesus, a radical rabbi from Galilee, rode a donkey down the Mount of Olives, cheered on by his peasant followers.

On the opposite side of the city, approaching from the west, Pontius Pilate, the Roman governor of Idumea, Judea, and Samaria, entered Jerusalem at the head of a grand column of imperial cavalry and soldiers.

Jesus's procession proclaimed the *power of the kingdom of God*; Pilate's proclaimed the *power of the Roman empire*. These two processions embody the central conflict of the week we reenact on Palm Sunday, the week that led to Jesus's crucifixion and the resurrection of Easter Hope.

Pilate's military procession was a demonstration of both *Roman imperial power* and *Roman imperial theology*. Rome was there to squelch likely uprisings, especially at Passover, the festival that celebrated the Jewish people's liberation from an earlier but similar empire.

The mission of Pilate's troops was to reinforce the Roman garrison permanently stationed in the Fortress Antonia, overlooking the Jewish temple and its courts. They and Pilate had come from the splendid new town of "Caesarea on the Sea," where they lived like royalty.

Imagine standing along one of those dusty cobblestone streets in Jerusalem that day, side-by-side with tradesmen, beggars, crying children, and praying women, when that massive display of imperial and military power burst upon the scene: cavalry on horses, foot soldiers, leather armor, helmets, weapons, banners, golden eagles mounted on poles, sun glinting on metal and gold. And imagine the sounds: the marching of feet, the creaking of leather, the clinking of bridles, the beating of drums, and the swirling of dust. Imagine the eyes of the silent onlookers: some curious, some awed, and not a few resentful.

Pilate's procession displayed not only *imperial power*, but also Roman *imperial theology*. According to this theology, the emperor was not simply the ruler of Rome, but the Son of God. It began with the greatest of the emperors, Augustus, who ruled Rome from 31 BCE to year 14 of the Common Era. His father was believed to be the god Apollo, who conceived him in his mother Atia's womb. Inscriptions refer to Augustus as "son of God," "lord," and "savior," one who had brought "peace on earth." After his death he was seen ascending into heaven to take his permanent place among the gods. His successors continued to bear divine titles, including Tiberius, who was emperor during Jesus's day.

For Rome's Jewish subjects, Pilate's procession embodied not only a *rival social order*, but also a *rival theology*. It was no surprise that Jesus's procession entered Jerusalem at the very same moment that Pilate entered. As Mark tells the story, it was a prearranged "counter procession," which Jesus planned in advance, a premeditated non-violent political demonstration.

The prophet Zechariah had envisioned it: A king would be coming to Jerusalem "humble, and riding on a colt, the foal of a donkey."[83] In Matthew the connection is explicit: "Tell the daughter of Zion, look, your king is coming to you, humble, and mounted on a donkey."[84] The rest of the Zechariah passage foretells what kind of king he will be: "He will cut off the chariot from Ephraim and the war-horse from Jerusalem; and the battle bow shall be cut off, and he shall command peace to the nations."[85]

Jesus's procession that day deliberately countered what was happening on the other side of the city. Pilate's procession from the West embodied the *power, glory, and violence of the empire* that ruled the world. Jesus's procession from the East embodied an alternative reality, the *kingdom of God's justice and peace*. This clash of empires—between the *Kingdom of God* and the *Kingdom of Caesar*—is central to the story of Jesus and early Christianity . . . and to our lives and our world today.

Jerusalem was the home of the glorious Temple of Solomon, a place of God's presence and God's forgiveness. But Jerusalem was also the center of an oppressive "domination system," a common way of organizing a society in order to control it. A "domination system" has three major features:

1. *Political Oppression*. In such societies the many were ruled by the few . . . the powerful and wealthy elites. Ordinary people had no voice in the shaping of their society.
2. *Economic Exploitation*. A high percentage of the society's wealth, which came primarily from the peasant's agricultural production, went into the coffers of the wealthy and powerful. And thirdly,
3. *Religious Legitimation*. These oppressive domination systems were justified with religious language. The people were told that the king ruled by Divine Right, the king was the Son of God, the social order reflected the will of God, and the powers that be were ordained by God.

The "ruling elite," about one to two per cent of the population, owned the land and controlled between one-half and two-thirds of the wealth produced by their society. The peasant classes who worked the land were constantly exploited by rents, taxes, and tribute. We call it the "normalcy of civilization," the political, military, and economic domination of the many by a few, and the use of religious claims to justify it. The *religious version* is that God has set society up this way; the *secular version* is that this is "the way things are" and the best they can be for everybody.

The contrasting form of society is a world of justice (and therefore peace) where, as the prophet Isaiah says, "They shall beat their swords into plowshares, and their spears into pruning hooks." A world where "nation shall not lift up sword against nation, neither shall they learn war any more."[86]

The prophet Micah adds: "They shall all sit under their own vines and under their own fig trees, and no one shall make them afraid."[87] These are images of justice, prosperity, and security . . .

Justice: where everyone will have their own land.
Prosperity: where vines and fig trees are about more than subsistence survival; and

Security: where they will not have to live in a state of common fear.

And all of this would come from a social order which gratefully acknowledged One Spirit, One Humanity, and One Earth.

The issue was not that the wealthy and powerful were "corrupt," if by that we mean an individual failing. As individuals, the wealthy and powerful were often good people—responsible, honest, hard-working, faithful to family and friends, interesting, charming, and good-hearted. The issue was not their individual virtue, but the role they played in the domination system. Were they exploiting others? Or were they empowering others by creating the opportunities necessary for them to lift themselves out of their conditions?

The larger question is, "At the end of the day, who is better off—the few or the many?"

As Jesus's procession drew close from the East and saw the great city of Jerusalem, he wept over it, saying, "If you, even you, had only recognized the things that make for peace! But now they are hidden from your eyes. Indeed, the days will come upon you, when your enemies will set up ramparts around you and surround you, and hem you in on every side. They will crush you to the ground, you and your children within you, and they will not leave within you one stone upon another, because you did not recognize the time of your visitation from God."[88]

Jesus was right. Jerusalem and the temple did not survive the first century. In 70 CE, Roman legions shattered the great revolt and tore down the temple. What survived was the Roman "domination system."

But what also emerged was a new Community of Faith which was focused neither on the social and economic domination of a few, nor on the exclusive religious privilege and domination of a few. "Whoever wants to be first must be last of all and servant of all," taught Jesus.[89]

Genuine discipleship, following Jesus then and now, means following him into the "Clash of Empires" . . . in Jerusalem as well as in America and around the world . . . to the place of ultimate confrontation with the domination system, as well as the place of death and resurrection. These are the two themes of awesome days Christians call "Holy Week." These are the two themes of the sacred life. These are the two themes of the salvation of the earth.

*   *   *   *   *   *

Two commanding processions entered Jerusalem on that day: a proud parade of Caesar's power, and a humble pilgrimage of Jesus's disciples.

Two triumphal personages entered the city gates that day: Pontius Pilate, an old kind of political hero of the Roman elite, and Jesus of Nazareth, a new kind of moral hero of the people of faith.

Two great empires clashed in the streets that day: the "domination system" and the "Kingdom of God."

Two great powers confronted one another that day: deadly power without justice, and lively power for justice.

And *two promised futures* were held in the balance that day: a world of equally-fearful "haves" and "have-nots" warring against one another for dominance over the earth . . . and a peaceful world of the children of God sharing all of life with one another.

That day is today! The same questions, the same allegiances, the same choices face those of us who would be faithful to God and our humanity today. Which procession are you in? Which procession do you choose to be in?

"What kind of day was it?" Edward R. Murrow would ask. "It was a day like all days, filled with those events which alter and illuminate our times." And you and I are there . . . today!

What choice will you make . . . today? It is my prayer that you will find Faith, Hope, and Love. And it is my earnest desire that with these gifts you will choose to live honoring Diversity and building Community and respecting all humanity regardless of the path they choose to enter into the realm of God. God speed to you in your journey.

EPILOGUE

SCREW DEATH, CELEBRATE LIFE

Gary wrote this while we were vacationing at our house in Baja California just after he had received his second opinion that he most likely had ALS. He would go to see Dr. Mitsomoto at Columbia University, Eleanor & Lou Gehrig MDA/ALS Center when we returned to New Canaan, Connecticut, at the end of August. Gary would then have more tests run, and we would be told in September, 2007, that, yes, Gary did have ALS. Gary lived each and every day from that point on as though it would be his last. His life teachings go on today; this is what he wanted. The Word Would Go On.

Bev Wilburn
March, 2011

* * * * * *

SCREW DEATH!

Man was made to live, not to prepare to live.

I will not let my life be taken over by some distant fear. I choose to live in this very moment. Nothing could be better than right here, right now.

Life is not lived in years or decades but in moments. Every moment is precious. Every moment is all we have. We live

99

momentarily. If I live this moment to the full, I have lived life to its fullest.

The past is past; the future does not exist. All we have is the present moment.

I now ask as St. Paul asked in I Corinthians, I think. Death where is thy sting, grave where is thy victory? The fear of death shall have no dominion over me. Everyone dies. Then life begins again.

Death, thou shalt die.

I will not live an unlived life.

It doesn't get any better than this. The waves are breaking on the beach. The ocean is blue-green with whitecaps popping up all over. The sea breeze is invigorating as it blows through my beach house. I can breathe here. I have reason to breath here. There are a thousand new beginnings here.

One white ship is moving north, another even faster is moving south. Everything is alive. Clear skies. Sea breeze blowing life through open doors and windows. Life is palpable. White gulls surfing the waves. Wind on the decks. Sun illuminating everything.

Everything is green. It is summer, but trees and gardens glisten against the white brick walls, the dusty cobblestone dirt roads, the mountains so close it seems you can touch them, and the deep blue sea.

If I died today, this is where I would want to be.

I've been told I have anywhere between 3 and 20 years to live. In a way, that's a gift. It causes me to value each moment. Physically I could live until I was 100 without the kind of love of life I have this moment, but I would not want to. The odds I have been given on the actuarial charts aren't all that great. But it has opened my eyes to living in the present moment. If I choose to do something, I will do it, and much is gained. If not, what's to lose?

How lucky I am. I am blessed with an unbelievable wife Bev, my true soul mate, who has been in my heart and at my side every one of our 38 years or so of marriage, and several years before that. No one could love another more than Bev has loved me, and continues to do so. Through all our life and into the next, I have loved her and cannot imagine myself without her. I have a fabulous son Sean, who no longer needs my coaching, who excels in everything I don't, who loves his mom and dad, loves his wife Joanie and his daughters, Isabella Rose and Cameron Grace. And I have a terrific daughter-in-law who is unbelievably right for Sean and a joy to us. Bev's mother, Wilma, is a strong anchor in our crazy tipsy/topsy world. Her husband Duane lives each day for itself. I'm sure I have a lot to learn from him. Her father Jack and wife, Fran, love each other and Bev. Mike and his wife Gloria are Bev's brother and sister-in-law. They also have learned to live each day to the fullest.

Throughout my life, I have been incredibly blessed with so many close friends and caring people. It would take my morning to list them all. Not only in California and Connecticut, but now in this fabulous beach community in Baja, Mexico, where we have been coming off and on for nearly 30 years.

Anyway, must go now. The Mexican water system is off again. I am working on my lectures for my class at church this fall, "The Faiths of Our Founding Fathers." I am very excited to learn more about the creation of our great country America from this unique perspective. Hope I can discover and communicate a few lessons for our chaotic world today. As filled as our forefathers' lives were with adventure, leadership, accolades, and dreams, I can't imagine any of these guys being as deeply happy and content as I am right now.

This is as good as it gets. And I couldn't want for more. Off to walk the beach in celebration of life.

—GARY
Baja California — La Mision
Wednesday, August 8, 2007, 10:00 a.m.

NOTES

FORWARD
1. The Principles of Progressive Christianity as developed under the leadership of the Reverend James Adams, founder and former president, and the Reverend Fred C. Plumer, the current president of the Center for Progressive Christianity (www.ProgressiveChristianity.org).

INTRODUCTION: Approach God Through Jesus
2. The Rev. James Adams, Founder, "The Center for Progressive Christianity" (Cambridge, MA), 1996-97 Report, p. 2. Information can be found at www.ProgressiveChristianity.org.
3. John 1:14
4. Marcus J. Borg, *Meeting Jesus Again for the First Time: The Historical and The Heart of Contemporary Faith* (San Francisco: HarperSanFrancisco, 1994).

JESUS AS THE MESSIAH
5. Marcus J. Borg, "Jesus Before and After Easter: Jewish Mystic and Christian Messiah," in Marcus J. Borg and N.T. Wright, *The Meaning of Jesus: Two Visions* (San Francisco: HarperSanFrancisco, 1999), p. 55.
6. N.T. Wright, "The Crux of Faith," in *The Meaning of Jesus: Two Visions*, ibid., p. 103.
7. N.T. Wright, *Christianity Today*, September 13, 1993.

JESUS AS THE LORD OF LIFE
8. William Sloane Coffin, sermon preached at The Riverside Church, New York, NY, April 11, 1982.
9. Walter Wink, "Resonating with God's Song," *The Christian Century*, March 23-30, 1994, p. 309.
10. William Sloane Coffin, *A Passion for the Possible: A Message to U.S. Churches* (Louisville, KY: Westminster/John Knox Press, 1993), p. 6.
11. Gordon Dalbey, "Does the Resurrection Happen?" *The Christian Century*, April 3, 1985, p. 319.
12. William Sloane Coffin, *Living the Truth in a World of Illusions* (San Francisco, CA: Harper & Row, 1985), p. 70.
13. "Thine Is the Glory," written by Edmund Louis Budry, 1884, translated by Richard Birch Hoyle, 1925.

JESUS AS A MOVEMENT INITIATOR

14. Marcus J. Borg, *Meeting Jesus Again for the First Time,* op. cit., pp. 30, 31.
15. Ibid., p. 31.
16. Luke 6:36
17. Marcus J. Borg, *Meeting Jesus Again for the First Time,* op. cit., p. 51.
18. Miroslav Volf, cited by Walter Wink, *The Powers That Be: Theology for a New Millennium* (New York, NY: Doubleday, 1998), p. 123, 124.
19. Walter Wink, ibid., p. 200.

JESUS AS A SOCIAL PROPHET

20. William Sloane Coffin.
21. Wilbur S. Stakes, Jr., March 6, 1999.
22. Amos 1:2, 3:8, 7:15
23. Marcus J. Borg, *The Meaning of Jesus: Two Visions,* op. cit., pp. 71 and 73.
24. II Corinthians 12:10
25. William Sloane Coffin, *A Passion for the Possible* (Louisville, KY: Westminster/John Knox Press, 1993), p. 58.

JESUS AS A WISDOM TEACHER

26. Robert Fulghum, *Maybe (Maybe Not): Second Thoughts on a Secret Life* (New York, NY: Villard, 1993), pp. 21-22.
27. My thanks to Howard Taylor, First Presbyterian Church of New Canaan member and chair of The Presbytery of Southern New England's Social Justice Committee, for his compilation of "sins" in the *Book of Confessions!*
28. Harry Emerson Fosdick, "Shall the Fundamentalists Win?" a sermon preached at the First Presbyterian Church, New York City, May 21, 1922. From Roger L. Shinn and Paul H. Sherry (ed.), *The Riverside Preachers* (New York, NY: Pilgrim Press/United Church Press, 1977), p. 37.
29. William Sloane Coffin.
30. Thomas G. Long, "Boxes and Breezes," *Pulpit Resource,* Vol. 27, No. 1, January-March 1999, p. 35.
31. William Sloane Coffin.

RECOGNIZE THE FAITHFULNESS OF OTHER PEOPLE

32. Adnan Pachachi, cited by Robert F. Worth, "Muslim Clerics Call For An End To Iraqi Rioting," *The New York Times,* Saturday, February 25, 2006, pp. A1, A6.
33. The Interfaith Alliance, Washington, D.C., February 2006.
34. Randall Terry, *The News Sentinel,* Fort Wayne, IN, October 16, 1993; U.S. Taxpayers Alliance Banquet, Washington, DC, August 8, 1995.
35. Gail R. O'Day, *The New Interpreter's Bible,* Volume X, (Nashville, TN: Abingdon Press, 1996), p. 745.
36. John 14:2

37. II Corinthians 5:19; I Timothy 4:10

38. John Shelby Spong, *A New Christianity for a New World: Why Traditional Faith Is Dying and How a New Faith Is Being Born* (San Francisco, CA: HarperSanFrancisco, 2001), p. 179.

39. Krister Stendahl, cited by James Adams, "Many Voices—One God?," President's Report, The Center For Progressive Christianity, Cambridge, MA, April 2001, p. 1.

40. John Shelby Spong, *A New Christianity for a New World*, op. cit., p. 182.

41. Point #4 of "The 8 Points of Progressive Christianity," www.Progressive Christianity.org.

42. Karl Rahner, cited by James Carroll, "Climate Change," *The Boston Globe*, May 17, 2005.

43. Point #6 of "The 8 Points of Progressive Christianity," www.Progressive Christianity.org.

44. Fred C. Plumer, Study Guide, "The 8 Points of Progressive Christianity," www.ProgressiveChristianity.org.

CREATION NON-SCIENCE

45. Romans 11:33

46. William Sloane Coffin, *A Passion for the Possible: A Message to U.S. Churches* op. cit., p. 64.

47. Balfour Brickner, *Finding God in the Garden: Backyard Reflections on Life, Love, and Compost* (Boston, MA: Little, Brown and Co., 2002), p. 132.

48. Cited by Barbara Brown Taylor, "Physics and Faith: The Luminous Web," *The Christian Century*, June 2-9, 1999, p. 612.

49. Simon Parke, *Origins: For Those Bored with the Shallow End* (New York, NY: Crossroad Publishing Co., 2001), p. 43.

50. Testimonials cited by Michael Reagan, *The Hand of God: Thoughts and Images Reflecting the Spirit of the Universe* (Atlanta, GA: Lionheart Books, LTD, 1999).

INVITE ALL PEOPLE TO PARTICIPATE

51. Robert Farrar Capon, *Hunting the Divine Fox* (New York, NY: Seabury Press, 1974), p. 90.

52. Paul Alan Laughlin, *Remedial Christianity: What Every Believer Should Know about the Faith but Probably Doesn't* (Salem, OR: Polebridge Press, 1999), p.75.

53. Marcus J. Borg, "Why Was Jesus Killed," *in The Meaning of Jesus*, op. cit., p. 80.

54. Marcus J. Borg, ibid., p. 81.

55. Alan Jones.

56. Krister Stendahl, *Energy for Life*, (Peoria, IL: Paraclete Press, 1999), pp. 90, 91

THE USE AND ABUSE OF THE BIBLE

57. Peter Gomes, *The Good Book* (New York, NY: William Morrow, 1996).

58. Colossians 1:27

59. I Timothy 4:10

60. Marcus Borg, *Reading the Bible Again for the First Time: Taking the Bible Seriously But Not Literally* (San Francisco, CA: HarperSanFrancisco, 2001), pp. 4-5. [Note: Borg references L. William Countryman's *Biblical Authority or Biblical Tyranny* (Harrisburg, PA: Trinity Press, 1994), pp. ix-x: These Christians (in the first group) imagine that the nature of biblical authority is perfectly clear; they often speak of Scripture as inerrant. In fact, however, they have tacitly abandoned the authority of Scripture in favor of a conservative Protestant theology shaped largely in the 19th century. This fundamentalist theology they buttress with strings of quotations to give it a biblical flavor, bit it predetermines their reading of Scripture so thoroughly that one cannot speak of the Bible as having any independent voice in their churches."]

61. Diana Eck, *A New Religious America: How a Christian Country Has Become the Most Religiously Diverse Nation* (San Francisco, CA: HarperSanFrancisco, 2002).

62. Ellen Goodman, "The Best and Worst of Religion," *The Los Angeles Times*, September 18, 2001.

63. William Sloane Coffin at a Pastor's Community Forum: "Homophobia in the Scriptures and in the Church," First Presbyterian Church of New Canaan, CT, January 12, 1997.

PREPARATION FOR DIVERSITY

64. Alice Miller, *For Your Own Good: Hidden Cruelty in Child-Rearing and the Roots of Violence* (New York, NY: Farrar, Straus & Giroux, Inc., 1983).

65. Martin Luther King, Jr., *Strength to Love* (Philadelphia, PA: Fortress Press, 1963), p.106.

KNOW THAT OUR BEHAVIOR REFLECTS OUR BELIEF

66. Jim Adams and Fred Plummer, from the original discussion contained in "The Study Guide for The 8 Points of Progressive Christianity," www.ProgressiveChristianity.org.

67. Ibid.

68. William Sloane Coffin.

TAKING CALCULATED RISKS

69. William H. Willimon, "Substance Abuse," *Pulpit Resource*, Vol. 24, No. 4, pp. 27-30.

70. Ibid.

71. Maureen Dowd, "Ted's Excellent Idea," *The New York Times*, August 8, 1996, Op-Ed Section.

NO MORE "SOUR GRAPES"

72. Thomas Howard, *Christ the Tiger* (Eugene, OR: Wipf & Stock Publishers, 2005).
73. William Shakespeare, *The Merchant of Venice*. Act 4, Scene 1, lines 193-197.
74. Arthur Leff, "Unspeakable Ethics, Unnatural Law," lecture delivered at Duke University, Durham, NC, 1979.
75. Ibid.
76. William Willimon.
77. C.S. Lewis, *Letters*, 18 July 1957, p. 276. Cited in *The Quotable Lewis* (Wheaton, IL: Tyndale House Publishers, 1989), p. 171.

IS PATIENCE A VIRTUE?

78. Patricia McCarthy, *Of Passion and Folly: A Scriptural Foundation for Peace* (Collegeville, MN: The Liturgical Press, 1998).
79. William H. Willimon, "Be Patient," *Pulpit Resource*, Vol. 23, No. 4, 1995, pp. 48-49.
80. Harvey J. Fields, "Cognitions On Two Condors," *Wilshire Boulevard Temple Bulletin*, Vol. 79, No. 5, February 3, 1992.

A CLASH OF EMPIRES

81. Garry Wills, "Christ Among the Partisans," *The New York Times,* OP-ED Section, Sunday, April 9, 2006, p. 12.
82. Marcus J. Borg and John Dominic Crossan, *The Last Week: A Day-by-Day Account of Jesus's Final Week in Jerusalem* (San Francisco: HarperSanFrancisco, 2006), p. 2. Note: This chapter makes use of extensive quotations from Chapter One of Borg and Crossan's book. With few exceptions, the words of the authors frame my argument and conclusion. I am indebted to Borg and Crossan for their fine service to the field of Biblical Studies and to my own faith.
83. Zechariah 9:9
84. Matthew 21:5
85. Zechariah 9:10
86. Isaiah 2:4
87. Micah 4:4
88. Luke 19: 41-44
89. Mark 9:33-35

ABOUT THE AUTHORS

The Rev. Dr. Gary Alan Wilburn was born in Seattle, Wash -
ington, on March 8, 1943, and was raised in Southern California.

Gary began his California ministry in 1963. After college he
worked with Youth for Christ in the San Fernando Valley area of
Los Angeles and later served as Director for the greater Long Beach
area. He served as youth pastor at Calvary Church in Pacific
Palisades, before attending Regent College, Vancouver, Canada,
earning the Master of Christian Studies degree in 1976. He served
as Associate Pastor at Bel Air Presbyterian Church in Los Angeles
from 1978-1988.

In the early 1980s Gary began to develop and share his core
belief that the gospel message is one of love, care, and compassion
for those in need. Gary inspired hundreds to make life-long com-
mitments to serve the poor and needy through an ecumenical
training program known as the HOPE Outreach. Appointed by the
Presbyterian Synod of Southern California to be a delegate to
South Africa during Apartheid, he preached about justice for all
people. Gary earned his Doctor of Ministry degree from Princeton
Theological Seminary in 1984.

Gary was called to serve as Pastor of the historic Immanuel
Presbyterian Church in the mid-Wilshire area of Los Angeles in
1988. He immediately encouraged a Saturday morning program to
help the youth of the area engage in and find opportunities in aca-
demics, athletics, and the arts. This program grew into HOLA, a
now independent program that continues to serve thousands of
inner city youth today. He also energized the Interfaith Mid-
Wilshire Clergy Association to meet the spiritual and physical
needs of the area and was recognized by them with several awards.

After the 1992 Los Angeles riots, Gary used his position as a cleric to mobilize volunteers to respond to the immediate needs of the community for food, water, and clean-up. He continued his efforts as a member of the mayor's committee for long-term solutions and rebuilding the communities devastated by the rioting.

In 1993 Gary was called to First Presbyterian Church, Stamford, Connecticut, as Interim Pastor. Two years later he was called to serve as Pastor of the First Presbyterian Church of New Canaan, Connecticut, where he remained until December, 2007. Under his leadership the New Canaan Church grew and remains a thriving, loving, and inclusive congregation.

As a member of the Interfaith Council of Churches and Synagogues of Southwestern Connecticut, Gary was instrumental in bringing together for the first time Islamic, Jewish, and Christian leaders to address regional and national issues of peace and justice. In 2001 they presented him the "Clergy of the Year" award partially in response to his interfaith work at the time of 9/11. He happily volunteered as the Chaplain of the New Canaan Fire Department. He spearheaded a project for the United Nations Day Committee of New Canaan to raise money to remove landmines from a village in Cambodia, only one example of his many charitable projects. Whether working in New Canaan or around the world, Gary was passionate in his commitment to disarmament and reconciliation.

Gary's 2007 diagnosis of Lou Gehrig's Disease (ALS) forced him to resign his pastorate, but it did not stop him from continuing to impact people with his message of hope and inclusiveness. During his three-year battle with ALS, Gary still insisted on living fully and with hope. He and Bev took this message with them as they moved to Playa La Mision, Baja California. There he wrote four books, the last compiled days before his death. Although confined to a wheel chair, he continued to grow his ministry, writing books and articles, starting Easter and Christmas services for the community in Baja, and hosting "Sundays with Gary," home gatherings to discuss life and faith issues. In spite of increasing physical limitations, Gary unreservedly engaged in the spiritual transformation of his new community. Gary was especially proud to be a national spokesperson for ALS Stem Cell Research.

Gary loved and lived life to the fullest from a spiritual center. His philosophy became the mission statement of the New Canaan Church: Live Spiritually, Love Inclusively, Learn Continuously, and Leave a Legacy. Gary's legacy will continue through the lives that he touched, inspired, and empowered to service.

Gary peacefully passed from the arms of his wife and son into the arms of God at his home in Playa La Mision, Baja California, Mexico, on June 28, 2010. Gary is survived by Beverly, his wife, best friend, and partner in ministry of over 40 years, and son Sean and wife Joanie, and granddaughters Isabella and Cameron.

Memorial Services to celebrate Gary's life were held at Bel Air Presbyterian Church, Los Angeles, at First Presbyterian Church of New Canaan, Connecticut, in his community at La Mision, Baja California, and at a private gathering of family and friends at his son's home in San Diego.

Gail W. Linstrom was born in Lakeport, California, and was raised in Carson City, Nevada. She graduated summa cum laude from the University of the Pacific, Stockton, California, with majors in English and Communication Arts. Upon graduation, she and her husband, Hugh, relocated to Los Angeles where she held various administrative positions. Her last office job was working for an optometrist with Bev until the Wilburns moved to Conn-ecticut, when she assumed Bev's position as office manager.

Gail has shared a long history with Gary, which began as a con-gregant and volunteer at Bel Air Presbyterian Church and where the two families became close friends. While Gary served as the Senior Pastor at Immanuel Presbyterian Church, Gail edited and published his weekly sermons for him. After Gary began to write, he contacted her about becoming his editor. With Gail's back-ground in English, it was a great collaboration and Gail discovered what she wanted to be when she grew up! She found it a privilege to assume more responsibility in helping Gary complete this last book.

Gail volunteers with several community groups and her church, where she is director of Adult Education and recently became a local ministerial candidate. In her spare time she loves to read, especially mystery and crime novels, knit, and travel.

Gail and Hugh have been married 40 years and have four grown children. Kendra, Bryan, and Andrew live in California; Anna and her husband Ben in Connecticut.

GARY WILBURN'S LEGACY

Gary believed deeply in "a faith beyond creeds, a humanity beyond borders, and a world beyond war." He worked tirelessly to make religion a uniting force that could confront and solve issues of poverty, ecological degradation, and war. He believed that there is beauty and strength to be found in our diversity and that it should be celebrated.

One of Gary's last projects was to help launch "One Word, One World," research currently being done at the Yale Divinity School's Center for Faith and Culture under the guidance of Professor Miroslav Volf, its Founder and Director. This project focuses on uncovering and exploring the ethical underpinnings that are shared by the world's religions and can be used to build bridges to solutions for world concerns.

As an adjunct to the Yale Project, the Wilburn Fellowship has been established in Gary's memory to award scholarships to high school students who propose meaningful projects that foster understanding of humanity's differences—whether of gender, race, ethnicity, nationality, creed, or culture—such that those differences can be respected, embraced, and celebrated, becoming the mosaic that binds and moves us forward in the community, the country, and the world.

Those wishing more information about these projects or wishing to donate to the causes can contact Warner K. Depuy, 84 Park Place, Stamford, CT 06901, or by email at warner@rhinopower.com.

Gary also considered his work as a member of the Advisory Board of the Center for Progressive Christianity (which recently changed its name to ProgressiveChristianity.org) an important contribution to this same world view. For more information about the Center's work and its goals to promote an understanding of Christian practice and teaching that leads to a greater concern for the way people treat each other than for the way people express their beliefs, the acceptance of all people, and a respect for other religious traditions, visit www.ProgressiveChristianity.org.

Additional Copies of this Book
and Gary Wilburn's Trilogy are Available

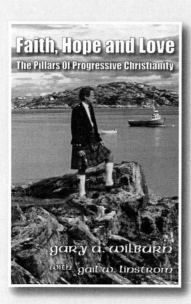

FAITH, LOVE AND HOPE: The Pillars of Progressive Christianity

I wrote this book to complement the Trilogy on Faith, Hope, and Love and to give you a roadmap for your faith journey. I wanted to challenge you to consider what a life lived according to the precepts of Progressive Christianity would look like, enriching you with all the diversity and beauty inclusiveness can bring to your life. Most of all I want you to live life to the fullest—as an adventurous journey loving your God with your whole heart, soul, and mind and your neigh - bor (and the whole world) as yourself.

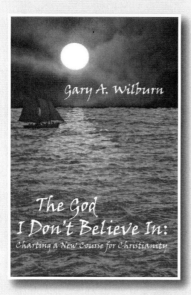

The God I Don't Believe In: Charting a New Course for Christianity

Here I explore my belief that we need to take a new look at our faith to find out what the Bible really says to us about how to think and act as Christians. In the upheaval of today, we wrestle with our faith or reject the faith of our youth because it seems irrelevant to the challenges we face. I invite you to embark on a journey of discovery to see if we can trans- form the 21st century to find A Faith Without Creeds ...A Humanity Beyond Borders ... and A World Beyond War—all because there is a God I do believe in.

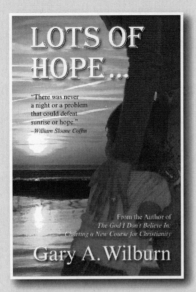

LOTS OF HOPE . . .

My intention is to give courage to those who live out their faith in ways that reflect how the world should be, not how it is, and to encourage others to do the same. I try to provide tools to put your faith into action today. The life of Biblical times is not the life we lead, but in some ways it is just the same. I address the challenges we face with examples from many perspectives by those in all walks of life. There are no easy answers, but I invite you to join the adventure fueled by the audacity of hope.

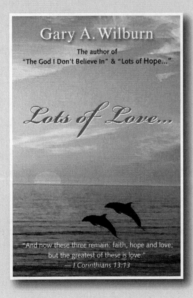

LOTS OF LOVE

Love is the beginning and the end of our journey. I want you to free yourselves from the fear that overrules your faith. Love may be a feeling, but it is expressed in very concrete ways. Our job is to discover our potential to change this world through the act of loving so we uncover the gift of life for ourselves and others. First I illustrate that love can be active even in the darkest and most challenging times. Then I share amazing and inspiring Christmas stories of the transformative power of the ultimate gift of Love.